Music and
Circle Time

Music and Circle Time

Using music, rhythm, rhyme and song

Margaret Collins and Claire Wilkinson

P·C·P
Paul Chapman
Publishing

First published 2006

 Paul Chapman Publishing
A SAGE Publications Company
1 Oliver's Yard
55 City Road
London EC1Y 1SP

SAGE Publications Inc.
2455 Teller Road
Thousand Oaks, California 91320

SAGE Publications India Pvt Ltd
B-42, Panchsheel Enclave
Post Box 4109
New Delhi 110 017

www.luckyduck.co.uk

Commissioning Editor: George Robinson
Editorial Team: Wendy Ogden, Mel Maines, Sarah Lynch
Designer: Nick Shearn
Illustrator: Philippa Drakeford

A catalogue record for this book is available from the British Library
Library of Congress Control Number 2006900705

ISBN 10 1-4129-1908-8
ISBN 13 978-1-4129-1908-1

Printed on paper from sustainable resources
Printed in Great Britain by The Cromwell Press Ltd, Trowbridge, Wiltshire

Contents

Introduction

The importance of music

The National Curriculum, Key Stage 1, Music, HMSO (1999) states that:

- Music is a powerful, unique form of communication that can change the way pupils feel, think and act.

- It brings together intellect and feeling and enables personal expression, reflection and emotional development.

- As an integral part of culture, past and present, it helps pupils understand themselves and relate to others, forging links between the home, school, and the wider world.

The National Curriculum, Music, states that:

Teaching should ensure that listening, and applying knowledge and understanding, are developed through the interrelated skills of performing, composing and appraising.

This is quite a tall order for Key Stage 1 teachers who are already burdened with the demands of the language, mathematics and science curriculum.

The National Curriculum, Music, asks teachers to involve children in:

- listening to music and sound

- responding to a range of musical and non-musical starting points

- performing

- composing

- appraising

- developing skills and understanding through a range of musical activities

- working on their own, in groups of different sizes and as a class.

Music should be a source of enjoyment and pleasure, that means fun, yet very young children are not able to listen for very long before becoming bored with inactivity. Can we integrate listening to music into the school day and use it to enhance other parts of the curriculum? There is no reason why music should not be playing while children engage in creative activities; perhaps a piece of music could be playing while children come into the classroom in the morning, when they are getting ready for lunch or getting ready to go home. Teachers can vary the kind of music from classical to popular and encourage children to bring in their favourite music tapes or CDs.

Many schools are using Circle Time as a venue for helping children to engage in discussion and listen to others. *Circle Time for the Very Young* (Collins, 2001) suggests that Circle Time could have a 'fun ending with songs, jingles and games.' This book seeks to encourage teachers to integrate music into the classroom by way of Circle Time and is designed to give you ideas of how to use music in the circle, both for fun endings and also as stimulation for further work.

Children need to be encouraged to listen carefully to music. They hear so much background music that no one really listens to. Only by encouraging them to really listen to a melody for a short spell will they begin to appreciate and develop a love for music. Just as children love to hear their favourite rhymes and stories over and over again, they will respond to pieces of music if they are given the opportunity to listen to the same piece several times and to learn its title, perhaps its composer and some interesting facts about the music.

Those of you who already use Circle Time will have laid down rules and strategies for ensuring that it runs smoothly. For teachers new to the technique of Circle Time, a list of resources is provided at the end of this book.

In this book we have tried to give you ideas for incorporating music into your normal teaching day and have in some cases suggested that you could use other stories or music to develop your own ideas. You will find that some of our suggestions lead you to think of other picture story books or pieces of music that you can use, either in Circle Time, in the classroom or in music lessons. It is only a starting point as teachers who are interested in allowing music into their classrooms will have more innovative ideas.

Perhaps, if you know any, you could invite musicians into your classroom. There will be children in your school or in your follow-on junior or middle school who are learning to play musical instruments. We suggest that you ask these budding musicians to play to the children in your class and perhaps they would be willing to talk about how they play their instruments.

We also suggest and give examples of where you can use music as a theme for art and craft work, for assemblies for other classes and for visitors.

The Qualifications and Curriculum Authority (QCA) makes the point that silence is important.

> Silence is a very effective part of making music. Children must be helped to recognise that in music all sounds are important and that silence helps to provide a clean sheet of paper on which the music can be created. www.standards.dfes.gov.uk/schemes2/music/mus07/07q5).

It is therefore very important that you help the children to appreciate silence and encourage quiet before the music begins and after it ends. They also say that, 'Silence is a vital part of any performance and may be the hardest part of achieve.' You will need to help children to learn to hold their instruments quietly or to put them down quietly in front of them when they are not required to play and to give lots of praise to those who achieve this silence.

There is considerable overlap as some of the ideas in the book could have been placed in more than one section; for example, in Section 1 some of the rhymes are also ring games and *Peter and the Wolf* has been used in two sections. Some of the tunes have also been used in more than one section. We hope that teachers will want to adapt some of the ideas in this book to other stories or themes and that the format we have used will help them to do this. It is hoped that teachers, especially non-musicians, will be inspired to bring their own knowledge of stories and music together to use in creative ways for the benefit of the children in their class.

Teachers will need to understand that some children may not want to show their work and may need encouragement while others may prefer not to demonstrate to the whole group what they have been practising.

Section 1: Rhythm, jingles, raps and chants

During Key Stage 1 pupils should be taught how to use their voices expressively by singing songs and speaking chants and rhymes… They explore and enjoy how sounds and silence can create different moods and effects.

The National Curriculum, Music, Key Stage 1.

In Circle Time, teachers often engage the whole group by asking them to finish the sentence or 'pass' the face or feeling. You can extend this with rhythm and music by asking children to beat out their sentences or singing their responses as in these activities.

Rhythm

At the end of a Circle Time session tell the children that you are going to clap a rhythm and ask them to copy it back. Start with something simple such as three slow beats. Ask the children to repeat this. Then use three quick beats and ask them to repeat it back to you. Vary the beats using slow and quick beats. Call it a 'follow my leader'; you beat the rhythm and they repeat it back to you.

Question and answer

Ask children to think of their own beating rhythm and beat this to the next child in the circle. That child listens, repeats the rhythm, then turns to the next child to beat her own rhythm, and so on around the circle.

Name rhythms

Ask the children to think of the rhythm of their name and go around the circle with a name question and answer. Start by you yourself clapping out your name, for example, 'Mrs Brown' (quick, quick, slow). Ask the next child in the circle to repeat their name and so on until everyone has had a turn.

Use the rhythm quick, slow, quick, slow as preparation for the next part of this activity. Clap out this sentence using your own name, starting with a quick beat and alternating with a slow beat… 'My <u>name</u> is <u>Miss</u>-es <u>Brown</u>.' (long beats underlined) Go around the circle with each child saying the sentence with their own name.

My family friend

Ask the children to think of a friend in their family and to think how their name would sound if they use this quick beat, slow beat rhythm. Vary the clapping by using two fingers of one hand beating into the other hand. Start by saying your own friend – perhaps use the name of your classroom assistant. Do this twice with a space in between, for example, 'My <u>friend</u> is <u>Miss</u>-es <u>Jam</u>-ie-<u>son</u> (pause). My <u>friend</u> is <u>Miss</u>-es <u>Jam</u>-ie-<u>son</u>.' Ask volunteers to beat out the name of someone in their family in this way.

Own rhythms

In Circle Time finish the session by using the focus of attention to make up a rhythm. For example, if you have been talking about healthy foods ask the children to think of some food they like to eat that is healthy and to make up a rhythm about it. You can start by saying, for example, 'I like milk to drink. What do you like?' The next child says what they like, for example, 'I like beans to eat. What do you like?'

After using and practising such rhythms you can ask the children to add song as in the following activity.

I helped someone

In Circle Time ask the children to think about something they have already done today which helped someone. Start by asking the children to join you in humming a nursery rhyme tune you all know well, for example, *Polly Put the Kettle On*.

Then use the tune and start a jingle by singing, 'I helped someone today when I …'

Finish this by adding, 'Got the painting things out for you.'

Ask the children if they can finish the jingle using other words.

Go around the circle, asking everyone for a response – but allow children to 'pass'.

I helped someone today when I shared my book with her.

Someone helped me

Ask the children to close their eyes and think of all the people who helped them this morning.

Ask them to hum to *I Had a Little Nut Tree*.

Think of a child who has helped you already this morning and start the jingle yourself by singing:

'Harry helped me today when he…'

Ask the children to work in pairs or very small groups and to choose the name of one person who helped them this morning and to try to make a jingle that will fit with the words. Come back into the circle and share their jingles.

I can be a friend

In Circle Time talk about the things you can do to be a good friend. Ask the children to work in pairs or small groups and make up a jingle to the tune of *Sing a Song of Sixpence*. Back in the circle ask each group to stand and sing their jingle. At the end of the session ask the children to think about the words in all the jingles. Can they choose the best bits from each and make up another jingle which best explains how you can be a

I can be a friend when I play a game with them.

I can be a friend when I share my things as well.

Playing well and sharing, helping them as well.

Aren't these good ways to show you care for all your friends?

good friend. Write this up and display it so that everyone can remember it. Perhaps children can help you to illustrate it.

Class poem chant

In the circle talk to the children about your class and the activities they like to do in your class. Ask them to finish the sentence: 'In our class I like to…'

Read them this class poem and help them to learn it.

In our class I like to paint.

> In our class we work and play
> Learn a new thing every day
> Reading, writing, numbers too
> Learning things is good for you.

Using four beats to each line, chant and clap the poem with the children and ask each of them to remember what they said they like to do in your class.

You could split the class into two and let one group beat four beats to the line and the other group beat each syllable. You could use instruments for a few children to play the four beats while others clap the syllables. At the end of each repetition ask volunteers to mime what they would like to do and ask other children to guess the activity. If you want to make a display ask the children to draw themselves doing what they like to do and display their drawings around the poem.

Partner rhymes

At the end of a Circle Time talk through the rhyme *Baa Baa Black Sheep*.

Divide the group into two halves with one half saying the first and alternate lines and the other half saying the second and alternate lines. Ask the children to move out of the circle and work in pairs facing each other, repeating the *Baa Baa Black Sheep* rhyme. In their pairs ask them to use other rhymes such as *Three Blind Mice* or *Cock a Doodle Doo, My Dame has Lost her Shoe*.

Question and answer rhythm

At the end of Circle Time ask the children to think of question and answer rhythms. Demonstrate this by finger beating and saying a question, for example, 'Is the sun shining today?' (You could use seven quick beats.) Talk about the answer, which will be either, 'Yes it is' or, 'No it isn't'. Go around the circle with each child asking this same question and the next child answering it. Ask the children to work in pairs, choosing their own question and answer rhythm. Back in the circle ask volunteers to demonstrate their rhythm to the class.

Rounds

When the children are used to partner rhythms, move on to four part rounds using songs or nursery rhymes they already know such as *Baa Baa Black Sheep*, *Half a Pound of Tuppenny Rice*, *Frere Jacques*. Stay in your circle and divide into four sections. You may need to have a 'leader' to stand inside the circle facing each quarter to help children to keep to their parts.

Enlist the children's help to make a class round which is relevant to your Circle Time theme.

Raps

Enlist the children's help in composing raps. Start by choosing a familiar story or poem, choose a beat rhythm and work as a class or in pairs to compose the rap. Here are three examples from well-known stories.

Princess rap

You could use claps and later introduce beating instruments.

Line five of the first three verses starts at a normal volume but gets quieter until line six is a whisper. The final verse is the opposite, with line five starting quietly and getting gradually louder until the final 'yes' is a shout.

There was a princess long ago
Who lived in a castle keep
The wicked fairy cast a spell
Which made her fall asleep.
Asleep, asleep (start loud, going quieter)
Which made her fall asleep.

There was a king lived long ago
Guard-ing the castle keep
The wicked fairy cast a spell
Which made him fall asleep
Asleep, asleep (start loud, going quieter)
Which made him fall asleep.

There was a queen lived long ago
She danced in the castle keep
The wicked fairy cast a spell
Which made her fall asleep
Asleep, asleep (start loud, going quieter)
Which made her fall asleep.

A handsome prince did then appear
He knew the forest well
He went into the castle near
And broke the witch's spell
The spell, the spell (start quiet and get louder)
He broke the witch's spell. YES!

Ask the children to add more verses in this style using other people who might be in the keep, for example, the cook, the coachman and the servant.

Red hen rap

When the children have learned this you could use claps or beating instruments to emphasise the rhythm.

You could choose one group to be hens and chicks, and the other to be ducks and pigs. Some could have instruments.

The little red hen said, 'Who will help?'
Said, 'Who, who? Who will help?'
The little red hen said, 'Who will help?'
As she worked in the sun all day.

The duck and the pig said, 'No not I,'
Said, 'No, no, no not I,'
The duck and the pig said, 'No not I.'
As they sat in the sun all day.

The little red hen said, 'Who will eat?'
Said, 'Who, who? Who will eat?'
The little red hen said, 'Who will eat?'
As she worked in the sun all day.

The duck and the pig said, 'Yes we will,
Said, 'Yes, yes. Yes we will.'
The duck and the pig said, 'Yes we will.'
As they sat in the sun all day.

The little red hen said, 'No you won't,'
Said, 'No, no. No you won't,'
The little red hen said, 'No you won't.'
As she worked in the sun all day.

The little red hen said, 'Come on chicks,'
Said, 'Come, come. Come on chicks.'
The little red hen said, 'Come on chicks.
Let's eat in the sun all day.'

The trip trap rap

Teach the children the words of the rap.

(&) (1) (&) (2) (&) (3) (&) (4)
Who's that go- ing ov- er?

(&) (1) (&) (2) (&) (3) (&) (4)
Who's that go- ing ov- er?

(&) (1) (&) (2) (&) (3) (&) (4)
Who's that go- ing ov- er?

(&) (1) (&) (2) (&) (3) (&) (4)
My Trip Trap Bridge

(&) (1) (&) (2) (&) (3) (&) (4)
It's li- ttle ba- by bi- lly goat

(&) (1) (&) (2) (&) (3) (&) (4)
Li- ttle ba- by bi- lly goat

(&) (1) (&) (2) (&) (3) (&) (4)
Li- ttle ba- by bi- lly on

(&) (1) (&) (2) (&) (3) (&) (4)
Your Trip Trap Bridge

Repeat with:

(&) (1) (&) (2) (&) (3) (&) (4)
It's mi- ddle sized bi- lly goat

(&) (1) (&) (2) (&) (3) (&) (4)
Its great big bi- lly goat

Then I'm going to eat you

(&) (1) (&) (2) (&) (3) (&) (4)

Then I'm going to eat you

(&) (1) (&) (2) (&) (3) (&) (4)

Then I'm going to eat you on

(&) (1) (&) (2) (&) (3) (&) (4)

The Trip Trap Bridge.

(&) (1) (&) (2) (&) (3) (&) (4)

No, I will fight and beat you

(&) (1) (&) (2) (&) (3) (&) (4)

I will fight and beat you

(&) (1) (&) (2) (&) (3) (&) (4)

I will fight and beat you on

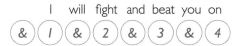

(&) (1) (&) (2) (&) (3) (&) (4)

Your Trip Trap Bridge

(&) (1) (&) (2) (&) (3) (&) (4)

Add body sounds

Troll – clap the rhythm as they say it.

Baby – tap the rhythm with one finger on their palm.

Middle – tap the floor with finger tips.

Great big - tap their thighs with palms.

Eat you – silence until 'eat you' when they use palms to slap the floor.

Fight you – knock with fists on the floor.

Percussion

Choose a pair or small group of children to play each instrument.

Use:

Verse 1: Troll – drum.

Verse 2: Baby – triangle.

Verse 3: Middle – chime bars.

Verse 4: Great big – tambourine.

Verse 5: Eat you – drum to play for these two words.

Verse 6: Fight you – drum, with everyone playing for the words 'beat you'.

Section 2: Songs

During Key Stage 1 pupils... sing a variety of songs from memory, adding accompaniments and creating short compositions, with increasing confidence, imagination and control.

The National Curriculum, Music, Key Stage 1

We suggest that you end your Circle Time sessions with a 'fun ending'. The songs in this section will help you to do that; they have a teaching purpose of their own as well as being fun. However, if you can link a song to the theme you are working on, so much the better.

There is a list of song books in the appendix.

Many children will know the following nursery rhymes which can form a fun ending to Circle Times.

Baa Baa Black Sheep
Boys and Girls Come Out to Play
Goosey Goosey Gander
The Grand Old Duke of York
Hickory Dickory Dock
Humpty Dumpty
Little Bo Peep
London Bridge
Michael Finnigan
Oh Dear What Can the Matter Be
Old Macdonald had a Farm
Oranges and Lemons
Polly Put the Kettle On
Pop Goes the Weasel
Sing a Song of Sixpence.

You can, of course, act them out to make it more interesting. Here are some suggestions for nursery rhymes and other songs.

Baa Baa Black Sheep

Choose characters – sheep, master, maid, little boy. Ask the sheep to kneel down and the rest to stand in the middle of the circle.

Line 1 – the master asks the sheep.

Line 2 – the sheep replies the second line.

Line 3 – sheep points to the master and maid, who bow or curtsey.

Line 4 – sheep points to the little boy, who runs around the inside of the circle.

You could also use percussion for the characters and choose other children to play.

Boys and Girls Come Out to Play

Choose three or four boys and girls to form two lines facing each other inside the circle. They act out the rhyme as below while the rest of the class clap or beat the rhythm.

Line 1 – boys and girls skip towards each other and back.

Line 2 – boys and girls make a circular movement with arms in air for moon.

Line 3 – boys and girls mime leaving supper and sleep.

Line 4 – join hand to make a circle and skip around.

The Grand Old Duke of York

All children stand up in the circle.

Line 1 – march on the spot to the beat.

Line 2 – hold up ten fingers to represent ten thousand men.

Line 3 – raise hands (fingers up) in jerks to the beat until hands are high in air.

Line 4 – lower fingers in jerks until at waist level.

Line 5 – fingers high, pointing to ceiling.

Line 6 – fingers low, pointing to floor.

Line 7 – fingers half-way.

Line 8 – fingers high for 'up' and very low for 'down'.

Humpty Dumpty

Line 1 – everyone sits up straight and tall (on the wall).

Line 2 – everyone falls over, curled up on the floor (a great fall).

Line 3 – everyone stands up and gallops on the spot (kings horses and men).

Line 4 – everyone mimes trying to put the egg together again.

You could act it out by splitting the class into three groups; eggs, king's horses and king's men.

You could use instruments or body sounds to suggest the actions, such as:

- slow claps or beating sticks to the rhythm of the first two lines
- jingle bells for line 3 (the king's horses)
- everyone playing or clapping for the last line.

Little Bo Peep

Lines 1 and 2 – everyone mimes looking, with one hand above eyes as they look.

Line 3 – everyone with palms upwards opens hands.

Line 4 – everyone on all fours as they mime a waggling tail.

You could choose a small group of sheep and a Bo Peep to act out the rhyme in the centre of the circle.

London Bridge

This is also a game which could be played by a few of the children in the centre of the circle, or if the group is small played by the whole group.

Oranges and Lemons

The children can mime to the actions. Ask them for their suggestions, or you could play it as a game with a small group of children in the centre of the circle or by the whole group if small.

Polly Put the Kettle On

Ask the children to work in pairs and to choose to be Polly or Sukey putting on and off the kettle as they all mime and sing.

Elephant Song (see appendix for notation)

Children stand up in their circle, choose one 'elephant' to go in the centre while the rest of the circle children turn into elephants by dangling one arm to nose to make trunk, the other arm flopping behind to form a tail.

Children walk around in the circle, their trunk holding the tail of the child in front.

Directions:

> Children walk around in one direction for first line.

One elephant went out to play

> Turn and walk the other way.

On a sandy beach one day

> Turn and walk the other way.

S/he had such enormous fun

> Stand and fact centre, clap to rhythm.

That s/he called for another elephant to come.

The first elephant in the centre chooses another elephant and the song is repeated as, 'Two elephants went out to play'.

The second 'elephant' chooses another and so on.

Carry on until you've had enough.

Variations

- If children keep choosing the same sex, alter last line to 'she' called for a 'bo-oy' elephant to come, or 'he' called for 'a gi-rl' elephant.

- When about half of the children are in the centre, change last line to: 'They all called for another elephant to come.'

If You're Happy and You Know It

Most children will know this traditional song. You could make it into a two group song, with one group doing the singing and the other the clapping, beating or playing an instrument. The children could work in pairs, with one doing the singing and the other the clapping.

Ask the children to suggest other verses to add, such as:

If you're sad and you know it, try to smile, don't cry.
If you're excited and you know it, share the fun, and smile.
If you're hungry and you know it, rub your tum, tum, tum.
If you're tired and you know it, go to bed.

Days of the Week (see appendix for notation)

Share this old rhyme with the children. Explain that it's about spending all week doing the laundry in days long ago and talk about how we use washing machines these days. You could use this rhyme when doing work on Victorians or mechanization.

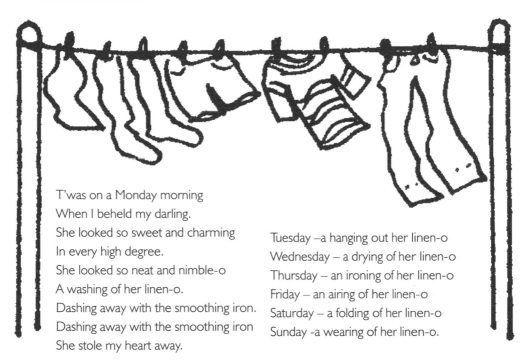

T'was on a Monday morning
When I beheld my darling.
She looked so sweet and charming
In every high degree.
She looked so neat and nimble-o
A washing of her linen-o.
Dashing away with the smoothing iron.
Dashing away with the smoothing iron
She stole my heart away.

Tuesday –a hanging out her linen-o
Wednesday – a drying of her linen-o
Thursday – an ironing of her linen-o
Friday – an airing of her linen-o
Saturday – a folding of her linen-o
Sunday -a wearing of her linen-o.

Help the children to compose a class song to this tune using the five days of the school week. Ask volunteers to suggest the things they do and jot down their ideas. You could start with:

> It's on a Monday morning, I come to school all yawning.
> I want to tell the things I've done all over the weekend.
> I tell about the fo-ot-ball, I tell about the swi-im-ming.
> Kicking the ball in the back of the net, etc.

There's a Hole in my Bucket

In Circle Time ask the children to think about what a bucket is and touch their ears if they can tell everyone. Choose a volunteer. Ask the children to finish this sentence: 'You can use a bucket to…'

Talk with the children about modern plastic buckets that we use today. Explain that in the old days buckets were made of metal and not thrown away when they had a hole in them, but mended with metal patches, not straw! Tell them that this is a fun song about a bucket with a hole. Sing the song through, letting the children join in with the repetition as they see the pattern.

When the children have learned the pattern of the song, either choose a group to be Liza and another group to be Henry or divide the class into two sets with one singing Henry's part and the other singing Liza's. You could ask those not singing to beat the rhythm.

> There's a hole in my bucket, dear Liza, dear Liza. There's a hole in my bucket, dear Liza, a hole.
>
> Then mend it, dear Henry, dear Henry, dear Henry. Then mend it, dear Henry, dear Henry, mend it.
>
> With what shall I mend it, dear Liza?…
>
> With straw, dear Henry…
>
> But the straw is too long, dear Liza…
>
> Then cut it, dear Henry…
>
> With what shall I cut it, dear Liza?…
>
> With a knife, dear Henry…
>
> But the knife is too blunt, dear Liza…
>
> Then sharpen it, dear Henry…
>
> With what shall I sharpen it, dear Liza?…
>
> With a stone, dear Henry…

But the stone is too dry, dear Liza...

Then wet it, dear Henry…

With what shall I wet it, dear Liza?...

With water, dear Henry…

In what shall I fetch it, dear Liza?...

In a bucket, dear Henry…

There's a hole in my bucket, dear Liza...

Sing about yourself

In Circle Time ask the children to think of something they would like to tell the group about themselves. Explain that you want them to put it into a song.

Ask them to finish the sentence: 'My song will be about...'

Explain that they can give their song a tune or it could be a song with rhythm and no tune.

Suggest song tunes they could use, all or part of tunes such as *Three Blind Mice, Twinkle Twinkle, Pop Goes The Weasel, Sing a Song of Sixpence,* to make the words fit.

> We are small.
> We like to play ball.
> We like to run and jump as well.
> We like to skip and jump as well.
> We are small, we like to play ball.

Send the children off in pairs or very small groups and ask them to think of the words they will use, add the tune and then practise singing or saying it.

Back in the circle ask for volunteers to sing their jingle.

Ask the children to write their jingle down and illustrate it.

Love your pets

(A variation of this song is in the instruments section.)

In Circle Time talk to the children about their pets and about animals they would like to have as a pet. Talk about caring for pets and what pets need.

Sing the first verse of *This Old Man* unaccompanied with the children.

> This old man, he played one,
> He played nick nack on my drum.
> With a nick nack paddywack, give a dog a bone
> This old man came singing home.

With a nick nack paddiwack, give your pet a stroke…

Ask the children to suggest variations for Line 3, such as

- give the bird some seed

- give your pet a stroke

- give your cat some food.

Doe a Deer, a Female Deer

You may have this song from *The Sound of Music* in your repertoire. It lends itself beautifully to work with chime bars. After singing the song and helping the children to learn the words (if they don't already know them), play for them the eight notes on chime bars, singing, 'Doh, ray, me' and so on as you play each note.

Choose eight children to stand in a line in the centre of the circle with one chime bar each in order. Ask them to play only the first note of each line.

Change children and ask the second group to play the beats of each line, four beats, while the other children sing.

As well as singing the words, the rest of the class can make a ring game out of the song, by skipping around the circle one way for the first line, changing direction for the next line and so on.

I Can Sing a Rainbow

You will probably have this song in your music collection.

> Red and yellow and pink and green
> Purple and orange and blue.
> I can sing a rainbow, sing a rainbow, sing along with you.
> Listen with your eyes, listen with your ears
> And sing every song you see.
> I can sing a rainbow, sing a rainbow, sing along with me
> Red and yellow, etc.

If you have children dressed in these colours, ask them to make a line in the middle of the circle to help other children remember the order of the colours. If not, you could provide coloured papers for children to hold. Perhaps you could ask children to paint pictures in only one colour so that these can be used.

You could ask only the children holding the colours to sing their own colour while the other children listen and join in with 'and' and sing the chorus altogether. You could make up a ring skipping game.

Five Little Fingers

This traditional finger rhyme is a good ending to a Circle Time session with the children suiting the finger action to the rhyme.

Five little fingers, long and thin (point both hands of fingers upwards)

Wave them, wiggle them, tuck them in (wave and wiggle fingers).

Five little fingers skipping around (fingers dancing on the floor or knees)

One crept away without a sound (hide one finger away).

Follow this with four, three, two, little fingers, with the last line of the last verse thus:

One little finger skipping around, can you guess what the finger found (all fingers come back)?

Children can draw around their hand with all the fingers showing.

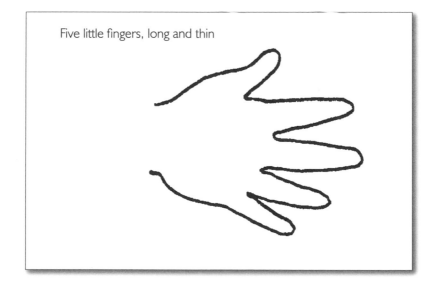

Five little fingers, long and thin

Section 3: Instruments

During Key Stage 1 pupils listen carefully and respond physically to a wide range of music. They play musical instruments and sing a variety of songs from memory, adding accompaniments and creating short compositions, with increasing confidence, imagination and control. They explore and enjoy how sounds and silence can create different moods and effects.

The National Curriculum, Music, Key Stage 1

Silence is a vital part of work with instruments. Children must learn to hold their instruments quietly when they are not required to play.

Qualifications and Curriculum Authority (QCA) 2000, Unit 6,
What's the Score? – Exploring Instruments and Symbols.

All children enjoy using musical instruments, not only for the beat but also for the quality of sound. Use the end of Circle Time to give the children the opportunity to create musical patterns, explore, choose and organise sounds and musical ideas, to work in pairs or small groups to make improvements to their own work.

Using instruments

These activities may take some time for all the children to have their turn, so you may need to limit each session by asking one group at a time to participate. The children will need time to practise their instruments and will need to know your rules about holding their instruments or putting them down in silence. You could ask the children to write their names on a list when they have had their turn with each instrument, making a running record.

Musical patterns

At the end of Circle Time, ask the children to work in pairs to beat out a simple rhythm, tapping their hands on their legs. Ask volunteers to show their musical pattern to the circle. Have available a small selection of instruments and ask these same volunteers to use one of the instruments to play their musical pattern. Ask the other children to try to remember their musical pattern so that they can have a turn with an instrument next time.

Choose your style

Using tuned and untuned musical instruments put one of each kind of instrument into the centre of the circle.

Talk about the different qualities of the instruments – the loud bangs of drums and tambours, the smooth sound of brush swirling on drum, the melodic sound of a glockenspiel and so on. Ask the children to think which instrument is most like them and to make one choice.

Ask each child in turn to finish the sentence: 'I think the... is most like me.'

Ask volunteers to go to the centre of the circle, choose their instrument and use it to repeat the sentence ('I think the ... is most like me.').

You can extend this activity by asking children to say why, for example, 'I think the triangle is most like me because it is quiet and gentle.'

A beating game

In Circle Time make sure everyone has an instrument and then ask the children to think of an animal they really like. Set up a gentle beating/shaking/tapping rhythm with the instruments. Introduce a space after each third beat. Practise this rhythm

A beating colour game

(Beat, beat, beat) Blue
(Beat, beat, beat) Green

and when the children have got it, go around the circle with each child saying the animal they like the best. It will go like this: (Beat, beat, beat) Dog, (Beat, beat, beat) Horse.

On other occasions change the children's contributions, for example, think of a colour you like, a person you like or a game you like to play.

Music your name

Again with only one of each of your instruments in the centre ask children to think of a rhythm for their name.

You choose one instrument and sing and play your name, for example, 'My name is Mrs Wilkinson.'

Ask each child in turn to go to the centre and beat or play their name with their choice of instrument. Some will like to sing their name at the same time.

Question and answer

This activity needs quite a lot of space – you may prefer to use hall time or go outside in the playground or garden.

Put all the instruments you have in the centre of the circle. Ask the children to work in pairs and think of which one instrument they would choose to use.

Before the children take their instruments ask them to think of a question and answer they could perform with this one instrument.

Demonstrate this with a child by choosing one instrument and singing a question using the instrument as back-up. Ask your child to answer.

It may go something like this:

'Which colour do you like best?' 'I like purple best.'

Ask pairs to choose their instrument and move out of the circle to practise this as quietly as they can. (You will need to organise this choosing, perhaps group by group.) Come together in a circle again and ask each pair in turn to play and sing their question and answer.

Story, song or nursery rhyme characters

You can use instruments to depict various characters from stories, songs or rhymes you know. Start by talking in your circle about a story you have recently shared. Ask the children to think which instrument is most like each character, thinking of how they move, their size or the pitch of the instrument. Ask for volunteers to be that character and play the instrument to show how the character moves and behaves. The following are examples and you will know other stories to use.

The Three Billy Goats Gruff

In the circle remind the children of the story, thinking about:

- how the troll could sound and act

- how each of the billy goats would sound, move and act.

Ask the children to work in fours – with each group choosing which of the characters to be. Depending on the size of your class you might need some groups to be three or five, with either an extra billy goat or one less.

We chose:

the drum for the troll

the tambour for the big billy goat

the tambourine for the middle sized one

the chime bells for the little one.

Ask each group to go outside the circle to talk about which of the instruments they would choose for each animal, and ask them to work out a sequence of events and movements.

Back in the circle, ask each group in turn to play out the story, using the instruments they have chosen.

Ask the children to draw and write about this lesson.

Cinderella

Ask the children to get into groups of six and to choose which of them will be each of the characters of the Cinderella story – Cinderella, three ugly sisters, Buttons and the fairy godmother. Tell the extract from the story where the three sisters won't let Cinders go to the ball, where Buttons tries to cheer up Cinderella and where the fairy godmother arrives.

Ask the children to think of which instruments would best describe each of these characters and how they would play the instruments to tell the story.

Allow the children to practise their movements both without and with the instruments.

Ask each group to perform their story in mime with only the instruments and their movements telling the story.

Jack and Jill

Ask the children to work in pairs to be Jack and Jill going up the hill for the water. Ask each child to choose two instruments – one for Jack and one for Jill. Ask each pair to go to a quiet area and make up a movement sequence using the instruments. After they have had time to practise, come back into the circle.

Mary chose the clappers for Jill and Zac chose the tambour for Jack.

Ask all the Jacks to stand and, in turn, to play their instrument.

Ask the Jills.

Ask volunteers to show their mime. If the children are happy to do this you may need to allow more than one Circle Time session.

(If you have more boys than girls, or if the children prefer to pair up with a child of the same gender, you can change the rhyme to Jack and Mick or Kate and Jill.)

This Old Man

Most children will know the words to this old traditional song, but you might like to personalise it for your children. Start with four beats to the bar, and clap or beat the rhythm as follows:

  (&) (/) (&) (2) (&) (3) (&) (4)

    This old man,   he played one

  (&) (/) (&) (2) (&) (3) (&) (4)

    He played nick nack on my drum

  (&) (/) (&) (2) (&) (3) (&) (4)

With a nick nack paddywack, give a dog a bone

  (&) (/) (&) (2) (&) (3) (&) (4)

    This old man came sing-ing home.

When the children have mastered the four beat rhythm, ask each child to choose an instrument, return to the circle and split the circle into four sets. Using the four lines of this verse ask each group to use their instruments while all children sing or chant the words, for example, for the first line the first group plays their instruments and the rest sing, for the second line the second group plays and the others sing, and so on.

Extension one – ask one group to beat the syllables with their instruments while the rest keep to the four beats.

Extension two – introduce a rest beat by breaking line one into two lines to make five lines, including a rest at the end of each line, thus:

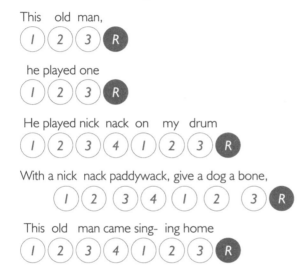

This   old man,
(1)(2)(3)(R)

he played one
(1)(2)(3)(R)

He played nick nack on   my   drum
(1)(2)(3)(4)(1)(2)(3)(R)

With a nick nack paddywack, give a dog a bone,
(1)(2)(3)(4)(1)(2)(3)(R)

This old   man came sing- ing home
(1)(2)(3)(4)(1)(2)(3)(R)

Chick, Chick, Chick, Chick Chicken

In Circle Time, perhaps at Easter, talk to the children about chickens and eggs. Do the children realise that eggs come from chickens? Talk about ways we use eggs – boiled, fried, in cakes, chocolate ones for Easter.

Sing the song to the children:

Chick, chick, chick, chick chicken, lay a little egg for me.
Chick, chick, chick, chick chicken, I want one for my tea.
I haven't had an egg since Easter, and now it's time for tea.
Chick, chick, chick, chick chicken, lay a little egg for me.

Split the circle into two parts and ask one part to sing the song and the other to clap the rhythm – three beats for each part followed by a rest, thus:

Chick, chick, chick, chick chicken

(1)   (2)   (3)   (R)

lay a little egg for me

(1)   (2)   (3)   (R)

(repeat these 2 lines)

I haven't had an egg since Easter

(1)   (2)   (3)   (R)

and now it's time for tea

(1)   (2)   (3)   (R)

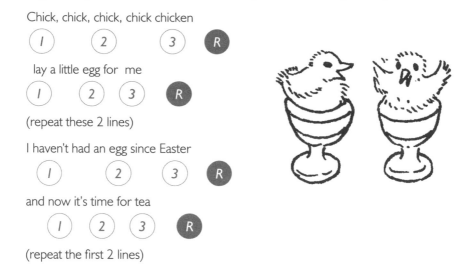

(repeat the first 2 lines)

Extension one – ask half the group to clap all the syllables and the rest to beat the above rhythm

Extension two – place enough instruments for one quarter of the class in the centre of the circle and split the class into four groups.

Ask each group in turn to choose an instrument to play the verse while the rest of the children sing.

Wake up Father Bear

(Silence is a vital part of work with instruments.)

This is a game using the characters from *The Three Bears.*

Sit in the circle, with a tambourine in the centre. This is the treasure. Choose a child to be Father Bear who hides his eyes or is blindfolded. In silence, point to a child who has to take the tambourine and hide it behind herself. Ask all the children to put their hands behind them. On your signal all the children chant:

'Wake up Mr Bear, your treasure is not there.'

Father Bear has three guesses as to who has the tambourine hidden behind them. Choose another Father Bear and repeat.

Ask for volunteers. You could either have one volunteer for each character with their instrument or several volunteers for each character either sharing an instrument or having one each. They could also enact part of the story. You may need to narrate the story or choose a narrator.

Children's own stories

After the children have had practice in the previous activities, ask each group of children to think of and make up a musical story with the same number of characters as there are in their working group, or half their working group if you have large groups of ten.

Give the children a few minutes to work this out and then choose the instruments they need. Give time for them to practise it and don't be surprised if it is very similar to a story you all know!

Older children could write their story.

Making use of hands

Make a bed from a palm, use two fingers as a beater and play about with rhythm. Start by all children beating a steady rhythm:

1, 2, 3, 4 steady beats.

Now clap the syllables of your school, for example, 'Radipole School' (quick, quick, quick, slow, pause). Ask all children to beat this.

Divide class into two halves and listen to one half beat the steady pulse, and listen to the rest beat the school name. Put the two together.

It could be useful here for each half to have a 'leader', either the teacher and a classroom assistant or two competent children.

Point out the two sounds at the same time – ask them what helps them to keep their pattern. (By saying words or counting numbers in their heads?)

Give all children (or each group of children) a drum, tambour or other skin instrument. Explore ways of using it, using hands only, tap, patter with fingers, scrape, etc. Return to two patterns previously learned (counting and school name). In two groups again, use the drums; listen to each group and then put them together. Repeat for fun and to improve. Change over groups.

Remain in the circle and allow the children to play any pattern they choose. Listen to one at a time, allowing children to 'pass'. (If you are short of instruments you may need to pass a drum around the circle.)

If all children have an instrument, tell them they are going to play their own pattern together.

Walk around the circle and point to one child at a time, indicating that they join in until all the children are playing their own pattern.

Move around again, pointing; this time the child stops playing until all are silent. Ask when the music is loudest and when it is quietest. Ask children to raise a thumb if they enjoyed the drumming circle.

Section 4: Movement

During Key Stage 1, pupils should be taught how to explore and express their ideas and feelings about music using movement, dance and expressive and musical language.

The National Curriculum, Music, Key Stage 1

Using musical language

You could introduce and use some of these musical terms during Circle Time:

Accelerando	Ac-sela-rando	Getting faster
Adagio	Ad-adg-io	Slowly
Agitato	Adg-it-ar-to	Agitated
Allegro	Al-eg-ro	Fast (literally, 'cheerful')
Andante	An-dan-tay	Quite slow (literally, 'walking pace')
Dolce	Dol-chay	Sweet
Forte	For-tay	Loud (literally 'strong')
Lento	Len-to	Slow
Piano	Pi-ar-no	Quiet
Pizzicato	Pit-zi-car-to	Plucked (instruction to stringed-instrument players)
Presto	Pres-to	Quickly
Scherzando	Scher-zan-do	Jokingly
Staccato	Stac-ar-to	Detached, separated (i.e. each note is sounded separately rather than slurred together with the following one)
Tranquillo	Tran-qui-llo	Tranquil
Vivace	Viv-ar-chay	Lively

New language

In Circle Time, explain to the children that there are special words for music, to help people to know how the music is to be played. Tell the children that 'piano' means quietly and 'adagio' means slowly. Ask them to stand up 'adagio' and 'piano'. Ask them to sit down 'piano'. Use both these terms in everyday work in the classroom.

Pass the face

Ask the children to 'pass the face' around the circle in a 'piano' way. Introduce 'presto' and ask them to pass the face in this way. Continue to introduce more musical terms in a fun way as the children recognise and remember them.

How will you move?

Make one card for each of the musical terms you have been using with the children; write one word on each card. At the end of Circle Time, show and read each card in turn to the children asking them to move in this way.

Shuffle the cards and place them face down in the centre of the circle. Ask a volunteer to take the first card, read it and move in that way. Can the rest of the children guess the word on the card?

Go to your place this way

Make sufficient cards for one per child and write on each card one word from the musical terms they already know. For example, piano, lento, adagio and presto.

At the end of Circle Time talk about the musical words they already know and remind them what they mean. Shuffle the cards and pass the set of cards, blank side up, around the circle, asking each child to take the top card. Ask them to read their card and think how they can move in this way.

Ask the children with the word 'piano' to stand and move in this way back to their classroom table, on the way putting their card in a pile on your table. Ask each group of children with another word to move in the way their card suggests to their place until all the children are in their places.

Can you guess?

Another fun ending to Circle Time is to use the cards you made for the above activity and pass them around the circle until each child has a card. Ask the children to hold their card face down, stand and move about the classroom in the way the card suggests until they find other people moving in the same way. Eventually the children will have formed groups moving in the same way. You can then stop them and ask them to move back to their places, putting the cards in a pile on the way.

Move this way

In Circle Time give each pair or small group a musical word, orally or on a card, and ask them to work together to make up a movement sequence using their word. Give them a few minutes to practise their movement and then return

We walk piano and andante at assembly time when we go in the hall.

We run presto in the playground.

to the circle. Ask each group in turn to show their movement sequence to the class. Can the rest of the children guess what their word is? Can they illustrate these musical terms?

How will Jack and Jill move?

At the end of Circle Time say or sing the nursery rhyme *Jack and Jill*. Ask the children to think about the ways Jack and Jill will move. Ask all the girls in the circle to stand up and show how they think Jill would move as she went up the hill. Can they give you a musical term for this? Ask the boys to show how Jack would move. Can they give a musical term for this?

Remind them of the way Jack came down the hill and ask a volunteer to come into the circle to show you how he did this. Can the children tell you the musical term? Ask the girls to think how Jill would have come down the hill, carrying the pail of water; ask a volunteer to come to the centre to show the group. What would this musical term be?

Use this idea with other nursery rhymes or with characters in the stories that you tell to the children.

High and low

At the end of Circle Time choose an instrument such as a guitar, glockenspiel, chime bars or recorder. Explain to the children that you are going to play a high or a low note and that you want them to listen to it carefully and put a hand up high if they think it is a high note and a hand down low for a low note. Bring in the fun element by asking them to make themselves tall for a high note and low for a low note.

What's your note?

At the end of Circle Time ask the children to number themselves, going around the circle, either 'one' or 'two'. The first child says 'one', the second 'two' the third 'one' and so on.

Using the tuned instrument as in the previous activity tell them that children with odd numbers are the low notes and the even numbers are the high notes. Start simply by playing alternate high and low notes, asking the children to move into star shapes (feet astride, arms high and apart) when they hear their note. Extend the activity by playing notes in random order, for example, 'one', 'one', 'two', 'two', 'two', 'one'.

More notes

Extend the previous activity the following Circle Time by adding an 'in between note', and ask the children to listen to these as you play the three notes going 'upstairs' and then down. Ask the children to number themselves around the circle, 'one', 'two' or 'three'. Tell the ones to stand and turn around and sit down whenever they hear their note. Tell the twos and threes to do the same action when they hear their notes. Start simply by going up the scale several times and then down the scale, giving plenty of time for the children to recognise their note and do the action.

Make more of a game of it by playing notes in random order. Play around with this idea by changing the actions or giving the three groups different actions to perform when they hear their note.

Weather

In Circle Time talk about the weather and ask the children to think of the different sounds that the weather makes. Ask volunteers to finish the sentence:

I think the rain makes a pattering sound.

'I think the wind makes a… sound.' Use different kinds of weather, for example, rain, snow, hail, sun, sleet, breeze, storm, blizzard and thunder.

Ask the children to move around the room in a careful way being the wind. Can they add sound to their movement?

Extend with other kinds of weather movements.

Moving like a drum

In Circle Time ask children to think about the musical instruments you have in school. Ask them to think first about a drum and to make their bodies into the shape of a drum. Sitting up again, ask them to think about how the sound of a drum might move around the room.

Ask two or three volunteers to come into the circle and show how they think the sound of a drum might move.

I think the shaking is red, like the sky at sunset.

Ask all the children to stay in their place, but move around in their body space as if they were the sound of drum.

Moving like a tambourine

In Circle Time ask the children to listen as you use a tambourine in several ways

– shaking, tapping, drumming. Ask them to close their eyes and tell you how each kind of sound makes them feel. Ask them to finish the sentence: 'The shaking makes me feel like…' Allow children to pass; repeat with tapping and drumming. You could ask volunteers, 'What colour do you think this sounds like?' Using tapping, shaking and drumming.

You could ask them to write and illustrate their feelings about the sounds.

Section 5: Ring games

> Pupils should be taught how to use their voices expressively by singing songs and speaking chants and rhymes.
>
> The National Curriculum, Music, Key Stage 1

It's fun to finish off Circle Time with a ring game as these give the children plenty of activity. Most children will be familiar with *The Farmer's in his Den, There was a Princess Long Ago, Here we Go Round the Mulberry Bush, Oranges and Lemons, Ring a Ring of Roses.*

In this section there may be a few you do not know and ideas for making up your own:

- Dusty Bluebells
- Big Bass Drum
- Looby Loo
- Grand Old Duke of York
- Get on Board
- Amy in the Ring
- Bingo
- Daisy Daisy.

In and Out the Dusty Bluebells

Ask the children to stand up in their circle and choose one child to start the chain.

The children hold hands and raise their arms to form arches. Then one child starts to go in and out of the arches and around the circle, while all the children sing the first three lines:

In and out the dusty bluebells

In and out the dusty bluebells

In and out the dusty bluebells

You shall be my partner!

For the fourth line the child stops behind the nearest child and taps them on their shoulder three times, while the others clap the beat of the rest of the song.

Pitter, pitter, patter on my shoulder

Pitter, pitter, patter on my shoulder

Pitter, pitter, patter on my shoulder

You shall be my partner!

The child who has been tapped on the shoulder goes behind the tapper and puts their hands around that child's waist.

The two of them go in and out the 'bluebells' until it is time to capture the next child to join the chain. The game ends when the chain is too long to go between the arches of the remaining circle.

Big Bass Drum

Practise in Circle Time with all the children sitting down and miming playing various instruments.

Put a selection of instruments in the centre of the circle and select one child to play the first instrument.

The rest of the children march, walk, skip or dance (according to the kind of instrument) around the circle miming to the instrument. After each verse the children pause while the child playing the instrument chooses another child to go into the centre to play the next instrument.

Oh we can play on the big bass drum
And this is the way we do it.
Boom, boom, boom goes the big bass drum
And this is the way we do it.

Oh, we can play on the violin
And this is the way we do it.
Fiddle-de dee goes the violin
And this is the way we do it.

Oh, we can play on the triangle
And this is the way we do it.
Ting, ting ting goes the triangle
And this is the way we do it.

Ask the children to select other instruments to make up other verses.

Looby-Loo

Children stand in a circle and hold hands. For the chorus the children sideskip around in the circle holding hands. They stop for the verse and perform the actions. Some teachers prefer to omit the last verse as this can lead to boisterous children causing accidents.

Chorus

Here we go Looby-loo

Here we go Looby light.

Here we go Looby-loo

All on a Saturday night.

Verses

Put your right hand in

Put your right hand out.

Shake it a little, a little

And turn yourself about.

Put your left hand in etc.

Put your right foot in etc.

Put your right foot out etc.

Put your whole self in etc.

The Grand Old Duke of York

This helps very young children to understand 'up', 'down' and 'half' as well as 'high' and 'low'.

Talk about the marching rhythm and link this to notation as a steady beat. Explain the steady 'left, right' marching rhythm that some children can play while others can play the whole song, with the 'twiddly bits' in it.

Experiment by clapping the marching beat with rests, only on the words:

'Grand', 'Duke', 'York' (rest), 'had', 'thou', 'men' (rest)

'marched', 'up', 'top' (rest), 'marched', 'down', 'gain' (rest).

Then clap the whole song slowly, clapping on each word.

Perform

Children in a circle march round, keeping to the circle with arms swinging.

'When they were up' – children stop and stretch up as high as possible.

'When they were down' – children stop and crouch down as low as possible
'When they were only half way' – children stop and crouch down half way.

Oh the grand old Duke of York
He had ten thousand men.
He marched them up to the top of the hill
And he marched them down again.

And when they were up, they were up.
And when they were down they were down.
And when they were only half way up
They were neither up nor down.

Use instruments within the circle

Choose a 'Duke' to play the marching beat on the drum for the first verse and a few other children with instruments, playing the rhythm for the second verse.

Get on Board the Train

This can fit in with a topic about transport or travel and would be particularly appropriate near a school holiday or a school outing.

In Circle Time talk about train journeys – how many children have been on a train? Count up a show of hands. Ask volunteers to talk about where they have been on a train. Play the ring game as follows:

Ask children to stand and widen the circle. The teacher chooses a train driver in the centre of the circle. Begin by tapping a steady beat with two fingers on a palm and step in time to it. Then add the chant with emphasis on the beats.

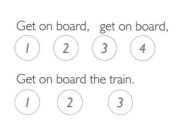

On the second repetition, the children chant softly while the train driver adds a name

Get on board, Jan-   et.
(1) (2) (3) (4)

Janet gets on board (puts hands around the driver's waist). Then Janet adds a name and so on until there is a train.

To extend this, the beat can be altered – faster, slower or change of emphasis.

Amy in the Ring

Use the once popular tune *Brown Girl in the Ring* (Boney M, 1970s) and sing or hum it with the children.

There are four lines.

> Amy in the ring, la la la la la
> Amy girl in the ring, la la la la la la
> Amy in the ring, la la la la la
> She looks for a boy with......

Ask the children to help you to make a ring game out of this tune.

Choose one girl to go in the middle of the circle and use her name for the song.

Line 1 – children skip towards the centre, stop for the 'la la la la la la'.

Line 2 – skip back, stopping for the 'las'.

Line 3 – as line 1; all children wait while the centre girl chooses a boy and sings.

Line 4 – 'She looks for a boy with...' and chooses some attribute such as brown hair, blue eyes, white teeth, curly hair.

All wait while the centre girl chooses a boy to replace her; everyone turns around as they go to make their original circle again.

The game continues with the boy in the centre, using his name, for example, 'Abdul in the ring'.

You may like to add actions for the 'la la' bit, for example, pointing a finger or swinging joined hands as in the 'hokey cokey'.

Bingo

Teach the children the words of the ring game.

> There was a farmer had a dog
> and Bingo was his name-o.
> B, I, NGO
> B, I, NGO
> B, I, NGO
> and Bingo was his name-o.

Ask the children to think of other verses, for example, a cat named H, E, NRY, or a mouse named S, A, RAH.

Ask the children to form a circle and choose one child to be the name and to stand in the middle.

Number the children, 'one' or 'two', and play the ring game like this:

Line 1 – all children skip to the right.

Line 2 – all children skip to the left.

Lines 3,4, 5 – children join up in pairs – a one and a two – cross hands and swing each other around.

Line 6 – re-form the circle and clap the rhythm.

Choose another verse and repeat.

If very young children find it difficult to join hands in twos and swing each other around, ask them to stand still and clap lines 3, 4 and 5.

You could explore the children's own names and those with five letters. Change the lines to read 'There was a farmer had a boy (or girl)'. You could ask the children to make a list of all the five letter names they know to add verses to this ring game.

Daisy, Daisy

Sing to the tune of *Daisy, Daisy.* (Amended version from one composed by Hiltingbury Infants School, Southampton, who gave permission for us to use this).

This song contains a useful sunsafe message to use in the summertime, before the children's school holidays.

Daisy, Daisy, playing outside is fun.

In the sum-mer it's lovely to be in the sun.

BUT

We mustn't forget our sun hats

And put on some cream, slip slap.

And if it's too hot, find a shady spot

Safe from the burning sun!

Line 1 – all children in the circle hold hands and side skip around the circle clockwise.

Line 2 – children sideskip anticlockwise.

Line 3 – children point into the centre.

Line 4 – mime putting on a sun hat.

Line 5 – mime putting on sun cream.

Line 6 – children turn around in their space with one hand above eyes as though looking for a shady spot.

Line 7 – children put outstretched fingers over head as though making shade.

You could use 'keeping safe in the sun' as a theme for Circle Time and extend the activity by asking the children to draw and talk or write about people playing safely in the sunshine. This activity would make a good theme to share with other classes or families during a class assembly. You could make a class book or wall picture showing children playing safely in the sunshine or shade.

Section 6: Music to listen to

You can give opportunities for listening to music by:

- choosing appropriate music for your Circle Time sessions and using Circle Time to talk about the composer, the composition, instruments and such like

- listening to a short piece of music at the end of Circle Time

- playing music in the classroom as children go about their normal learning

- organising pre-assembly music with pictures, posters and information about the music, the composer, any story about the music and time of composition.

In Circle Time

There are many suitable pieces of classical music with a strong memorable theme that you can use as well as occasional pieces of modern music. Share some of the classical composers' works as well as music you yourself love. Brief information about some composers can be found in the appendix.

As well as using music as a fun ending to Circle Time you could use a piece of music as the focus. Listen to a small part of the melody and talk about the music, the composer, the reason for the composition and the instruments used.

This music made me feel happy and want to smile at everybody.

Ask children to work in pairs to compose a short movement sequence and ask for volunteers to show this to the circle.

Following Circle Time, ask children to illustrate the theme of the music or to use mixed media to produce illustrations of how the music makes them feel.

Extend the children's learning by displaying books about the music, composer or instruments. Encourage children to ask their families to help them to find out more about the composer or work. Ask them to bring their findings to the next Circle Time session.

You could share this work with others in your year group or in whole-school assemblies.

Assemblies

Appreciation of music can be shared with all the school if daily assemblies use the same music each day when the children come in to assembly and take their places. If you have a circle formation for assembly you can encourage the children to take part in the music part of assembly by asking questions such as:

- What does this music make you think about?

- How does this music make you feel?

- What kind of picture inside your head does this music make for you?

- What describing words can you use about this music?

You could choose a different piece of music for each week, introducing it on Monday. You could make a simple illustrated visual aid showing the title, composer and a brief note about the music, perhaps using the record sleeve, if it is a record. Each morning the children's attention could be directed towards the poster and music.

You can use some of the Circle Time strategies at the beginning or end of assembly, for example, by asking the children to:

- 'pass the face' that best describes how the music makes them feel

- 'touch their nose' if the music makes them feel happy

- 'touch their ears' if they can name one of the instruments playing

- 'touch their elbows' if they have heard the music before.

For example, if you used the music *Pictures at an Exhibition*, you may like to do some of the following:

- use this music for the whole term as the assembly music.

- introduce each piece on a Monday and ask children to draw pictures to display alongside the visual aid you have made

- ask each class to take one of the themes to further explore

- find out about the composer, Modest Petrovich Mussorgsky.

Start by listening to the main recurring theme, the Promenade. In assembly, ask these questions:

- How does this music make you feel?

- What do you think is happening when this music plays?

- What pictures does this music make in your head?

Explain that the music tells the story of the composer walking around an exhibition of pictures in an art gallery and stopping in front of various pictures before walking on to view the next picture.

In class Circle Time give children the opportunity to talk about how the promenading music makes them feel by finishing the sentence: 'The promenade music makes me feel…' Ask the children to walk around the room as though they were walking around an exhibition of pictures, stopping before each one.

Listen to and explain each of the 'picture' themes in turn, over a period of several days, giving opportunity for discussion and appreciation of the relevance of the music to the picture.

After listening to the whole of the music ask each child to draw their impression of one of the pictures and make an exhibition of your own.

Mussorgsky, Modest Petrovich (1839-1881), one of the most original and influential of the 19th-century Russian composers, was almost self-taught.

He composed the piano suite, *Pictures at an Exhibition* in 1874. For more information see: http://russia-in-us.com/Music/Opera/mussorgsky.html

The Clog Dance

Use *The Clog Dance* (1789) from the ballet *La fille mal Gardee* by Ferdinand Herold.

If possible, find and conceal:

- a pair of clogs
- a picture of people wearing clogs.

(See appendix for story of the ballet.)

In Circle Time, listen to the music once through without telling the children the title. Ask the children to touch their ears if they think they have heard it before. Ask volunteers to tell the class about this.

This music made me think of happy people dancing in the street.

Ask them to finish the sentence: 'This music made me think of…' Jot down their responses.

Ask them to finish the sentence: 'This music made me feel…'

Show the children the clogs and your picture of clogs and talk about them as footwear worn by work people years ago and the sound the clogs made on the pavement stones. Talk about clogs worn in Holland and how blue and white pottery clogs are often made there as a kind of symbol of that country.

Ask the children to work in pairs to make a short movement sequence relating to a piece of the music. Encourage children to show their movement to the circle.

Play the music again and ask children to beat out the rhythm with their fingers on the floor. Ask them to hum the melody. Ask them to choose and describe the bit they like the best.

Teachers who don't know this music can get help from the website www.ballet.co.uk/contexts

Coppelia

Stories that composers have used to compose their ballets could be read to the children in Circle Time (see resources at the end of the book). Short selections from the music can be used in the classroom for children to listen to and become familiar with.

You can isolate parts of the music and use these small pieces as a stimulus for movement as well as asking children to listen to the rhythm and use the beat in their own compositions.

Read or tell the story of *Coppelia*, using a story book or the synopsis on page 84. Ask the children to re-tell you the story from the beginning and make a note of the important incidents in the story. Write down this précis. Identify five or six short pieces of music that tell these scenes, for example:

- the dance sections, when the chorus of villagers dance
- the excited music when the girls of the village discover the dolls in Dr Coppelius' workshop
- the jerky music when the clockwork dolls begin to move
- the scary music when Dr Coppelius returns
- the happy ever after music at the end of the story.

On the following days end Circle Time by playing one short piece and remind the children of that part of the story. Ask them to think about how this piece of music makes them feel. Ask them to finish the sentence: 'It makes me feel…' and give them time to move to the music before they go on to their next activity.

Once the children know the main musical themes you may like to use a whole lesson period for them to dance the story to the short pieces you have selected. You could extend this by casting children as characters in the story and telling the story as the children dance each section.

Ballet stories lend themselves to art work and the making of classroom collage pictures. You could use this work as preparation for a class performance to other classes or as part of an end of term concert.

See website http://www.radacadabra.org/coppelia.htm

Section 7: Music and art projects

> Children should be taught the knowledge, skills and understanding through responding to a range of musical and non-musical starting points…
>
> The National Curriculum, Music, Key Stage 1

After listening to and talking about music help children to express the music and how it makes them feel, using paint, crayons, collage or pastels.

Information and websites about the stories, music and composers can be found in the appendix. Most schools will have picture storybooks in their library or these can be obtained from local lending libraries.

In this section we look at how music makes us feel and the kinds of pictures it paints for the children.

There are suggestions for using the following pieces of music:

Firework Music

The Sorcerer's Apprentice

Romeo and Juliet

Peter and the Wolf

The Sleeping Beauty

The Trout

How does it make you feel? What picture does it paint?

A good starting point is to choose a piece of music that has a strong melody and storyline. After listening to the music and talking about it in Circle Time ask the children to think about how it makes them feel. Ask them to close their eyes and see what kind of picture it makes inside their heads. Ask volunteers to answer open-ended questions such as:

- What kinds of feelings does it make you have?

- What colours does this music make you think about?

- What kind of things could be happening?

- Where is it happening?

- What kind of picture does it make inside your head?

> This *Carmen* music is all red and fast and exciting. It makes me think of people being busy at Christmas time.

With the music playing ask the children to illustrate what they see or how it makes them feel. You may like to do this by setting up an art area for one group at a time or by having a whole class art session with all kinds of media available.

The following examples may give you more ideas.

Firework Music (George Frederick Handel)

This is appropriate for the autumn term with links to 5th November.

In Circle Time listen to excerpts of the music with the children.

Introduce the project by making a starter visual in the form of an illustrated poster or small display using the record sleeve or a picture and any books you have in the school library.

Tell the children that Handel wrote this music for King George I to celebrate a peace treaty. On May 15th 1749 the music was performed for the King on the River Thames in London.

Ask the children to close their eyes and make a picture in their heads of musicians playing as boats process down the Thames with all the pageantry and ceremony this would have entailed.

Ask volunteers to give you words to describe how this makes them feel.

If you can, provide some of the instruments for the children to examine and pass these around the circle. If not, use pictures to help the children to understand how they are played.

Explain that you want the children to help you to make a large class picture of the procession of the boats down the river, with musicians playing. After Circle Time ask children to help you to make a background for the picture. Ask them to draw colour and cut out boats, people and musicians to add. Help the children to include fireworks in their class picture.

This music made me feel excited and I could see pictures of the fireworks in my head.

The Sorcerer's Apprentice (Paul Abraham Dukas)

Introduce the project by making a starter visual in the form of an illustrated poster or small display using the record sleeve or picture and any books you have in the school library.

In Circle Time tell the children that this music is based on a ballad by a German poet and that Paul Abraham Dukas wrote this music to tell the story of the sorcerer and his helper. In Circle Time listen to the music and tell the children the story of the music. Explain what sorcerers and apprentices are.

Select appropriate excerpts and ask the children to think about how they could tell the story through the music with movement.

Ask the children to move freely to the music with all of them being the sorcerer, the apprentice, the broom or the magic spells.

Give children plenty of opportunity to explore the different roles then choose several apprentices and brooms but one sorcerer. Ask the rest of the children to be the magic music as it swirls and comes to a climax.

Artwork

Prepare a large background for a picture story, with several sections. If you choose three sections, you could have the first one showing the apprentice working with the sorcerer and the spell book, the second showing the devastation as the apprentice invokes the magic and the third showing the final entrance of the sorcerer. Ask the children to make (with paint, paper and junk materials) the sorcerer, the apprentice, the brooms, musical notes and magical symbols. Help them to assemble the collage(s) of figures and brooms, littering it with notes and symbols.

Ask the children to write:

- about the magic spell
- an account of the event as if they had been there
- the composing of the music
- their own movement or dance.

I think the apprentice would have felt very worried when the brooms kept on coming.

Celebrate the finale of the project by sharing this work with the whole school in an assembly, with parents or another class to see the picture, read the writing and watch your movement interpretation of the music.

Romeo and Juliet (Peter Ilyich Tchaikovsky)

Introduce the project by making a starter visual in the form of an illustrated poster or small display using the record sleeve or picture and any books you have in the school library.

The Romeo and Juliet Overture was composed by Tchaikovsky. His music is well-known for its richly melodic evocation of the moods of the stories on which they are based. (See appendix for more information about Tchaikovsky.)

Tell the children a simplified version of Shakespeare's tragic love story about two families who could not be friends. Ask the children to think what could be done to unite these families – what would they say to the two 'houses'?

Listen to the music – you could have a tape or CD in the classroom that children could choose to listen to when doing other work. Pick out short sections for movement.

Ask the children to tell the story in their own words and work in groups to make pictures of the various scenes and display as a strip picture. Mount children's writing about the music and story to put alongside the pictures they have drawn. Use them to extend your starter visual.

Shakespeare

The tragedy *Romeo and Juliet* (c.1595) is famous for its poetic treatment of young love; it tells the story of two lovers who were victims of the feuds and misunderstandings of their families and by their own hasty temperaments.

For the story and photos of the ballet, see website:www.radacadabra.org/romeojuliet.htm

Peter and the Wolf (Sergei Prokofiev)

(See Section 8 for another project on this theme.)

In Circle Time, start by reading a version of the story (see Appendix 2). Explain how the characters are each given a different instrument to represent them. Listen to short extracts of the music.

In several Circle Times select one character's music and ask the children to move to it. When the children can recognise the different parts of the music, select and play excerpts to help them to 'tell the story' through movement.

Class pictures

You could:

make a large background of a woodland and ask the children to draw, paint or use fabrics to make the characters to stick onto the background. The final part of the story with the procession of all the characters would make a good picture or make a background with several sections, such as:

- The cat creeping up on the duck.

- Peter didn't listen to his Grandfather and went out into the meadow. He saw the wolf and managed to catch him with a rope.

- Grandfather telling Peter to stay away.

- The wolf appearing and catching the duck with the cat up the tree.

- The bird flying down to anger the wolf with Peter in the tree.

- Peter pulling up the wolf by his tail.

- The huntsmen marching to the rescue.

- The final procession.

Label each section of the story and ask the children to create the characters to add to it.

Ask the children to write their version of the story to display around the big picture.

Find out about the composer and display this information near the picture.

The Sleeping Beauty (Peter Ilyich Tchaikovsky)

Introduce the project by making a starter visual in the form of an illustrated poster or small display using the record sleeve or picture and any books you have in the school library.

In Circle Time, tell the children the story of the sleeping beauty – you can finish Circle Time by playing the ring game *There was a Princess Long Ago*.

In the following Circle Time, listen to parts of Tchaikovsky's music – or play it softly in the classroom while the children are doing their activities. Explore excerpts of the music in movement sessions.

Break up the story into sections, for example:

The sleeping princess pricked her finger and slept for 100 years.

- the christening
- the bad fairy's arrival
- the 16th birthday party
- the spinning wheel
- the sleep
- the prince cutting down the hedge
- the awakening.

Ask all the children to choose to illustrate one of the sections, using any media. Collect all the pictures for each section of the story and vote which picture of each scene to display in order to put together and make a long picture story.

Ask children to write a sentence or two to put under each picture and choose a different person's writing to caption each picture.

Add written or illustrated descriptions of the music together with information about the composer.

The Trout (Franz Schubert)

Schubert wrote this song in 1815 and in 1819 composed the *Trout Piano Quintet*. It was named this because the slow movement is a set of variations on the theme of the song *The Trout*.

Introduce the project by making a starter visual in the form of an illustrated poster or small display using the record sleeve or picture and any books you have in the school library.

In Circle Time listen to the slow movement with the children and ask them to close their eyes and try to make pictures inside their head of a trout swimming up river.

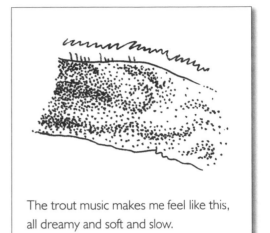

The trout music makes me feel like this, all dreamy and soft and slow.

Listen to the music again and ask the children to work in pairs or threes to make up a movement sequence that fits in with the main melody. Ask volunteers to show their movement/dance to the whole class.

Ask the children to close their eyes and again visualize the movement of the trout before asking them to use paint to express their feelings about the music.

Ask the children to write a report or caption about their paintings and display some of these together alongside your starter visual.

Section 8: Story and music projects

During Key Stage I children should be responding to a range of musical and non-musical starting points.

They should work on their own, in groups of different sizes and as a class.

The National Curriculum, Music, Key Stage I

This section contains examples of how stories and music can be used to extend children's musical awareness. A list of resources is provided at the back of this book.

Peter and the Wolf
Gassire's Lute
Handa
The Wild Swans
Going on a Lion Hunt
Goldilocks
The Gingerbread Man

Peter and the Wolf

You could use four lessons for completion. (See also Section 7 for an art project on this theme.)

You will need:

- a storybook of *Peter and the Wolf*
- a tape, CD or record of the story
- various instruments
- poster of instruments for the children to refer to
- large cards for children to draw symbols.

Lesson 1

In Circle Time tell or read the story to the children.

Explain about the instruments that are used for the various characters:

- Peter – the strings

- Bird – the flute

- Cat - the clarinet

- Duck – the oboe

- Wolf - French horn

- Grandfather - the bassoon

- Huntsmen – the drums.

Listen to the music extracts, showing the pictures of the instruments as each is played. If you have access to older children (or adults) who play musical instruments invite them to come and play to the children.

Explain how instruments are grouped together in an orchestra.

Lesson 2

In Circle Time, remind the children about the previous lesson and explain that today they are going to be various characters in the story. First ask all children to turn themselves into a wolf and prowl around the circle. Follow this with them being a bird, then a duck and cat.

Ask children to sit down again in the circle and to suggest a school instrument to represent each animal. Tell them that you are going to be the wolf and they will be the other animals.

Form three groups, with each group representing one animal (bird, duck, cat) with the chosen instrument. Ask the children if this is how an orchestra would be arranged.

Ask the children to think of how they would play their chosen instrument if they were flying like a bird, swimming like a duck, creeping like the wolf or climbing like a cat. Ask each group in turn to practise playing their instrument as though they were each animal moving in this way.

You yourself use the drum to represent the wolf. Play it in different ways and ask the children to suggest how the wolf would be moving, for example, fast would suggest running and quietly and slowly would suggest stalking.

Lesson 3

Before the session, ask the children to draw some of the characters. Label these characters and use a class instrument to represent each character.

In Circle Time listen to the extract where the bird and duck argue. Remind the children of the school instruments they used in Lesson 2 and ask them to work in pairs, to be a bird or a duck and have a musical argument using those instruments.

Choose pairs to perform to the audience.

Lesson 4

This lesson will help children to understand how symbols are used to represent sound. You'll need a set of seven A4 cards to draw symbols to represent the instruments the children will use for each character.

In Circle Time remind the children of the previous sessions and explain that they are going to play all the characters in the story.

Divide the class into seven groups; each group to have a different instrument, one for each character, for example, the tambour represents the wolf.

Give each group a card on which to draw a symbol for their instrument and place this where all the children can see. You will need to re-make the circle, perhaps with children two deep, with a small space between each group and space for you to stand, either inside the circle or at a central point where everyone can see you.

As you tell the story, use the cards to ask the children to 'play', for example, when you say, 'Grandfather called out', point to the grandfather card with the symbol and children with those instruments will play their instruments. You will need to set a hand signal for the end of their playing so that you can get on with the story!

Gassire's Lute

See website for pictures and information about lutes: www.vanedwards.co.uk/history1.htm

Use 'Encarta'; search for lute, click 'multimedia' and listen to the sound of two different lutes.

Music has an important role in many parts of Africa as it once was an integral part of the life of Africans from birth. At a very early stage in life the child used to take an active role in music, making musical instruments by the age of three or four. Musical games played by children used to prepare them to participate in all areas of adult activity – including fishing, hunting, farming, grinding maize, attending weddings and funerals and dances.

In Circle Time, read *The First City of Wagudu* from *Stories from West Africa* by Robert Hall, or tell this abridged version.

Many years ago a legendary tribe came from the north and settled along the River Niger in West Africa where they built a great city called Wagudu. One day invaders came and great and terrible battles raged as the people of Wagudu tried to protect their city and people.

The King of Wagudu had grown old and Prince Gassire and his sons were fighting to save the city. Gassire went to see the Wise Man to ask what would happen and the Wise Man said, 'You will never be King. The city will fall, but your song will live for ever.'

Gassire thought about this strange prophesy and called for the instrument-maker to bring him a lute but when he fingered the strings the lute played no tune. The instrument maker said that the lute was silent because it had no heart or experience and told Gassire to take it to battle with him.

The battle raged and many warriors were killed and their blood fell upon the lute. Soon all Gassire's sons except for the youngest had been slain and the rest of the people came to Gassire and begged him to end the fighting and leave the city to the invaders so that there would be peace.

Sadly Gassire and his son, with a few friends, left the city and wandered into the countryside. The legend says that as they sat around their campfire they heard the lute begin to sing the story of Wagudu. The song told of the greatness of the old city and the battles where so many had fallen. It told of sand covering the fallen stones of the lost city of Wagudu. It also sang about the peace of the fields and the song of the birds.

Activities

Explain to the children that a lute is a bit like a guitar with a long neck and a pear shaped body, with strings that can be plucked with the fingers of one hand or played with a plectrum. The lute was introduced to Europe in the tenth century and became very popular during the Renaissance. Today lutes are usually used in folk music.

Talk about legends, songs and stories becoming part of the history of a nation. Remind them that before people could read, their history was carried through generations through song, poems and stories.

Ask the children to finish the sentence: 'The part of the story I liked is...'

Ask younger children to help you to write down the song of the legend, re-capping the essential parts of the story with a short sentence. Ask older children to work in pairs to compose a song about the feelings of Gassire when he had to leave the city to his enemies.

Listen in Circle Time. If you can find a CD with lute music on, listen to it, or use the Encarta multimedia sound on your classroom computer. Perhaps you could make a tape recording of both the sounds to listen to in Circle Time.

When I hear the sound of the lute it makes me feel all jerky and tingly inside me and my shoulders want to rock.

Ask the children to close their eyes as they listen and then to tell you what they felt as they heard the music, finishing the sentence: 'I felt...'

Divide the class into four or five groups and ask them to practise acting out the part of the story where the lute begins to play the song.

Handa

Drums used to be the most common instrument throughout rural Africa; every village would have had one or more. Each village would have had a master drummer. In many African languages the word 'drum' means 'dance'. Drums were used to make contact with the ancestors, to communicate over long distances and to accompany every celebration.

You will need:

- *Handa's Surprise* or *Handa's Hen* by Eileen Browne or other book about Africa
- drums or other beating instruments.

Music to listen to:

- *Master Drummers of Africa*, Kopano, ARC Music Production UCD 1631.

In Circle Time put all drums and tambours in the centre of the circle.

Read the book you have selected. Talk about the life and celebrations of children who live in communities such as this. Ask the children to finish the sentence: 'I think living in Africa would be…'

Drumming activity

In Circle Time, start by asking the children to clap hands and repeat this rhythm; clap, clap, pause; keep going until all the children can hold the beat. Change to…

Tap knees, clap hands, clap hands; pause; repeat.

Tap floor, clap hands, clap hands; pause; repeat.

Then alternate, clap floor, clap, clap, pause; clap knees clap clap.

Improvise and change the pattern, for example, floor, floor, knees, knees.

Increase and decrease the tempo.

What is a drum?

Ask children to close their eyes and think about the shape, what it is made from, how it is played and ask them to finish the sentence: 'A drum…'

Explain that we should never put a drum flat on a surface to play because this will block the sound. It should always be tilted or held between the knees.

Show the children how to play the drum with a flat hand using different parts of the surface. Listen to the different sound made when using a hand on the centre, further out and the rim.

Put all your drums, tambours etc. in the centre of the circle and give children time to collect and share these and experiment by using their flat hands on drums.

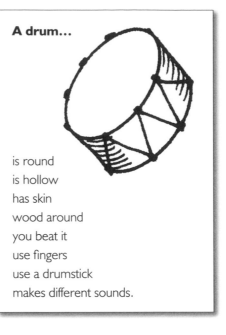

A drum...

is round
is hollow
has skin
wood around
you beat it
use fingers
use a drumstick
makes different sounds.

The Wild Swans

Use *The Swan* from the *Carnival of the Animals* by Saint-Saens.

Read the synopsis of the story in the appendix or read a picture story book such as *The Wild Swans* by Hans Christian Anderson.

Tell the story in one Circle Time and do the activities in another.

Set the scene

In the circle ask children to rub their palms together and whisper:

- flying swans, flying swans – repeat
- beautiful swans, beautiful swans – repeat
- magic swans, magic swans.

Listen to the music of *The Swan*.

Talk about the tempo and the feel of the music.

Listen again, this time asking the children to close their eyes and draw in the air as they listen.

Percussion

Use chime bars and xylophones and ask each child to choose an instrument for flying music.

Play – does it sound right?

Choose another instrument to represent the human princes.

Play – does it sound right?

Talk about and compare the two kinds of music they have created.

Ask children to work in pairs, one to be the swan prince and one to be human. Ask each pair to select appropriate instruments and to practise together.

Talk about the tone of the two pieces of music they are making.

The swan prince music must be gentle, piano/adagio.

The prince music must be lively, presto/allegro.

Ask each pair to join another pair and work out a pattern of music with now two swan princes and two human ones.

Ask a volunteer group to show the other children their music.

Conclusion

Ask all the swan princes to sit together in one half of the circle and the human princes to sit in the other.

Re-tell the section of the story where the swan princes fly over the sea, stop on the island and fly on, so that the two groups play alternately. Allow enough time for them to play their patterns.

Ask them to play their music without you telling the story. This should be a repeated sequence. You could end with fading out. Give your music a name and perform to another class.

Extension

Make music about Elisa in various stages of the story, for example, when she is cast out of the castle, meeting the swans, marrying the king, condemned as a witch or rescued by the princes.

You may like to ask the children to make a class strip picture depicting the main scenes of the story

Going on a Lion Hunt

Most schools have versions of this story (sometimes it's a bear hunt by Michael Rosen). These activities use *We're Going on a Lion Hunt* by David Axtell. Read the story in a previous lesson. Use voice to say the words and hands on parts of the body to make sound.

Introduction

In Circle Time ask the children to establish a steady beat with hands on the floor to represent an elephant plodding, 1,2,3,4.

On hands and knees chant, then pause while beating:

> We're going on a lion hunt (beat with hands on floor 1, 2, 3, 4).

> We're going on a lion hunt (beat again 1, 2, 3, 4).

Repeat until everyone joins in and is excitedly waiting for what's coming next.

Learn the chants as they are repeated with different sounds.

> We're going on a lion hunt (pause voice and beat 1, 2, 3, 4).

> We're going to catch a big one (pause voice and beat 1, 2, 3, 4).

> We're not scared (pause voice and beat 1, 2, 3, 4).

> Been there before (pause voice and beat 1, 2, 3, 4).

> Can't go over it (hands going over).

> Cant go under it (hands going under).

> Can't go around it (hands going around).

> Have to go through it (hands moving forwards).

Remain in the circle, chant and 'sound' the story.

Verse 1

> We're going on a lion hunt…

With two palms together do actions for the next section…

> Oh no! Long grass…

> Can't go over it…

> Swish, swash, swish, swash (make sounds by rubbing sleeves on front of jumper).

Verse 2

Repeat chant:

> We're going on a lion hunt…

> Oh no, A lake…

Repeat:

> We can't go over it…

Make sound by rubbing hands together and making 'splish splash' vocal sounds.

Verse 3

Repeat chant:

> We're going on a lion hunt…

> Oh no, A swamp…

> We can't go over it…

Repeat using voice – 'squish squelch, squish squelch'.

Verse 4

Repeat chant:

> We're going on a lion hunt…

> Oh no, a big dark cave…

Repeat:

> We can't go over it…

> Have to go through it.

> In we go, tiptoe, tiptoe.

Use fingers of one hand to pitter patter on the other.

Verse 5

> But what's that?…

> One shiny wet nose

> One big shaggy make

> Four big furry paws

> It's a lion!

Scream (quietly).

Back out through the cave by moving back a little to make a larger circle, and reverse the actions quickly as the hunters return through the swamp, lake and long grass until they are home.

Extensions

Use instruments.

Give out enough instruments, one for each child in the circle, to use for the 1, 2, 3, 4 instead of beating the floor. Ask the children to think which instruments could represent the long grass, lake, swamp and cave. Group the circle into four sections and give each section a different type of instrument to play instead of 1, 2, 3, 4. While they are playing their verse, the other three groups whisper or quietly tap 1, 2, 3, 4. Come out of the circle and start at one side of the room, moving slowly towards the other side as you meet the obstacles. Choose a small group of children to play the instruments as the others go on the journey.

In each case, once the lion is spotted repeat the verses quickly in reverse order, speeding up until everyone is safe home again.

This story would also lend itself to a class story book. Write up the sections you choose to have illustrated and ask each group or pair of children to choose one section and to illustrate this on A3 paper. Make a cover and staple together to make a large class book.

Goldilocks (in two or more sessions)

You will need:

- the names of instruments to be used printed on A4 cards

- various instruments of your choice

- music for the song *When Goldilocks went to the House of the Bears* from the book *Oranges and Lemons* or other publications

- activity sheet for each child; a piece of A4 ruled into two columns with spaces for character and instruments, see page 75.

Lesson 1

In Circle Time read or tell the story of *The Three Bears*.

Get into the music mood by tapping or clapping the following rhythm:

Gold – i- locks – slap knees on 'Gold' and clap for the two other beats.

Reverse the process, clap for 'Gold' and slap knees for the other two beats.

Teach *When Goldilocks went to the House of the Bears* to the children adding appropriate actions, for example, touching eyes for 'blue eyes', indicating size for the bears.

Ask the children to describe the characters in the song – to choose one character and finish one of the sentences:

'I think Father Bear would be...' (or Mother Bear, Baby Bear or Goldilocks).

Look at the classroom instruments and ask the children to think about which instrument would fit itself to each character. How would it be played? For example, bells are perhaps not suitable for Father Bear, but might suit Baby Bear.

Describe Father, loud, slow, angry. Could this be played on a drum?

Put one of each kind of instrument in the centre of the circle. Ask volunteers to label the instruments, using the cards provided.

Father Bear would be loud, heavy, slow, angry. You could use a drum.

Mother Bear would be soft, gentle, loving, you could use a tambourine.

Ask the children to choose which instrument they think is best for each character and to complete the activity sheet by drawing and labelling each character and instrument. They can do this on the floor in the circle or at their table.

In the circle, ask volunteers to show their activity sheets and to say why they chose each instrument. Sing the Goldilocks song, with actions and instruments.

Lesson 2

You will need:

- instruments
- low screen to hide instruments behind
- some of the completed activity sheets from the last session.

In Circle Time sing the Goldilocks song with actions.

Look again at, and talk about, one or more of the activity sheets from the previous session and vote on which instruments the class will choose for each character.

'Who's that? game

You choose three instruments suitable for the bears, for example a drum for Father Bear, maraca for Mother Bear and triangle for Baby Bear. Ask the children to say why they think you have chosen these instruments. Play each instrument and ask them to remember which character it represents. Hide the instruments behind a screen and chant:

Who's that walking in the woods today?

Who do we hear?

You play one instrument and ask children to call out the name of the bear it represents.

Once the children have learned the game, ask a child to go behind the screen and play one of the instruments.

Another game

From the previous lesson pick a few of the best instrument selection activity sheets and put children into groups of four. Ask them to find the instruments and, using them, to practise walking (andante) in the woods, creeping up the stairs (adagio) and chasing Goldilocks (presto). Give each group time to compose a movement sequence to their instruments and ask volunteers to go to the centre of the circle to show their sequence to the whole class.

Follow the story

Give one or two groups of four children a set of instruments. Ask them to sit in the centre of the circle and play at the appropriate time. The rest of the children stand in the circle and move around in one direction only. Read out a brief story outline involving these three aspects so that the children can play instruments during the story.

One morning the three bears went out for a walk while their porridge cooled. (Groups play all the three bear instruments as the rest walk around circle.)

On their return they realised that someone had been in their home. They crept around. (Children play instruments at creeping tempo (adagio). The rest of the children creep around the circle.)

Fast asleep was a little girl who woke suddenly and ran from the house. (Children in the circle stand still and listen.)

The bears chased her away. (Group play all instruments (presto) as the rest of the children run around the circle.)

Beat a drum loudly twice for silence.

Back in the circle all together, talk about the different ways they have played their instruments and moved around the circle.

Draw the character **Draw the instrument**

Goldilocks	
Father Bear	
Mother Bear	
Baby Bear	

The Gingerbread Man

In Circle Time tell or remind the children the story of the Gingerbread Man. There are many versions and this story will be in the school if not the class library. A short synopsis is in the appendix.

Help them to learn the phrase:

Run! Run!

As fast as you can.

You can't catch me

I'm the Gingerbread Man!

The lilt of this is well known. Still in the circle, with the whole class, beat this rhythm using hand claps and adding percussion instruments such as claves and wood blocks. When this is established, move on to three parts, with:

> Run, (rest), run, (rest),
>
> as fast as you can, (rest)
>
> you can't catch me,
>
> I'm the Gingerbread Man

1. Group one beating or clapping the whole verse.

2. Second group clapping or beating 'Run! Run!' over and over again.

3. Third group clapping or beating 'Gingerbread Man' over and over again.

Once you have established this rhyme and rhythm introduce two chime bars, C and G.

Demonstrate:

- playing C for 'Run! Run!'

- playing G for 'As fast as you can.'

One child could play two chime bars.

Break into small groups and ask children to experiment with instruments and body music before rehearsing their favourite.

Ask various groups to play the verse as someone tells or reads the story again.

Appendix 1:

Notes on the lives of some well-known composers

Ludwig van Beethoven 1770-1827

Beethoven was born in Bonn, Germany in 1770 – his birthday is thought to be on December 16th. His father was a musician and he was very stern with Ludwig, making him learn to play and compose. When he was 19 the young Beethoven began supporting his family as a court musician.

It was planned that Beethoven should study in Vienna with Wolfgang Amadeus Mozart. Although Mozart's death (1791) prevented this, Beethoven went to Vienna in 1792 and became a pupil of the Austrian composer Joseph Haydn where Beethoven dazzled the aristocracy with his piano improvisations; at that time he was thought of as Vienna's finest pianist.

When he was 30 years old he realised he was beginning to lose his hearing and so began to compose music instead of playing it.

In the *Pastoral Symphony* Beethoven tried to create images of the countryside with sounds of water and birds.

More information at: www.mfiles.co.uk/composers/Ludwig-van-Beethoven.htm

Frederic Chopin 1810-1849

Chopin was born near Zelazowa Wola, near Warsaw, Poland. His father was French and his mother Polish.

Chopin began to study the piano at the age of four and composed pieces before he knew how to write them down. Chopin was only eight years old when he played at a private concert in Warsaw.

The piano, at that time, was a new and modern instrument and beginning to replace the harpsichord. Chopin was an extraordinarily gifted pianist and preferred to play in the homes of rich and important people rather than in concert halls. The music he wrote contains many melodies from Polish folk music.

In 1831, Chopin went to live in Paris, where he became noted as a pianist, teacher and composer but in 1838 he began to suffer from tuberculosis and spent some time in Majorca in the Balearic Islands.

After 1847 his musical activities were limited to giving several concerts in 1848 in France, Scotland and England. He died in Paris on October 17 1849, of tuberculosis.

More information at: www.mfiles.co.uk/composers/Frederic-Chopin.htm

Paul Abraham Dukas 1865-1935

Dukas was born in Paris. He composed *The Sorcerer's Apprentice* in 1897, basing the music on a ballad by the German poet Johann Wolfgang von Goethe.

Among other works by Dukas are the overture *King Lear* (1883), the ballet *La Péri* (*The Genie*, 1912) and the *Sonnet de Ronsard* (1924) for voice and piano.

More information at: www.kontek.net/uc/music/Sorcerer.htm

George Frideric Handel (1685-1759)

Though Handel was German by birth, in 1727 he became a naturalized British subject. He came to England in 1710, returned to Hanover and was granted permission for a second, short trip to London, from which he never returned. In 1714 the Elector of Hanover, his former employer, became King George I of England and he appointed Handel to be music master to the king's children.

He wrote music for the church and for royal celebrations. *His Music for the Royal Fireworks* was composed to celebrate the peace treaty in Aix-la-Chapelle in 1749. On the 27th April, 1749 it was performed in Green Park, London, where it is said the fireworks failed to go according to plan but the music was a great success. Another firework display was given on 15th May 1749 on the Thames in presence of the King.

More information at: http://en.wikipedia.org/wiki/George_Frideric_Handel

Louis Joseph Ferdinand Herold (1791-1833)

Herold was born in Paris on the 28th of January 1791. He studied at the Paris conservatoire. He then moved to Italy where he composed music.

His more important works were *La Clochette* (1817), *Marie* (1826), and the ballets *La Fille mal Garde* (1828) and *La Belle au bois Dormant* (1829).

Herold also wrote a lot of piano music, in spite of his time being much occupied by his duties as accompanist at the Italian opera in Paris.

In 1831 he produced two operas which secured immortality for the name of the composer. He died on the 18th of January 1833 of the lung disease from which he had suffered for many years, and the effects of which he had accelerated by incessant work.

More information at: http://71.1911encyclopedia.org/H/HE/HEROLD_LOUIS_JOSEPH_FERDINAND.htm

Wolfgang Amadeus Mozart (1756-1791)

Mozart was born in Salzburg, Austria. It is said that playing Mozart's music for children to listen to as they come into assembly has a calming effect on them.

When Mozart was three years old he began to try to play the pieces his seven year old sister was learning to play on the harpsichord (an instrument similar to the piano).

When he was four he learned to play the violin perfectly and when he was six he wrote a concerto.

It was at this time that Mozart's father decided it was time to show off his talented children. He took them to the great cities of Europe – Paris, London, Prague and Vienna. They became known as the 'wonder children'.

Mozart wrote more than 800 pieces of music, sometimes playing from memory because he hadn't had time to write it down. He was always short of money as people gave him gifts instead of paying him for his music.

Some of his greatest operas were *The Marriage of Figaro*, *Don Giovanni* and *The Magic Flute* (first performance in 1791).

He died that year, when he was 35 years old.

More information at: www.mfiles.co.uk/composers/Wolfgang-Amadeus-Mozart.htm

Modest Petrovich Mussorgsky (1839-1881)

He is thought by some to be one of the most original and influential of the 19th-century Russian nationalist composers. He was almost self-taught. The folk songs he heard as a child inspired him to improvise at the piano even before his mother started teaching him. He was educated in Saint Petersburg and was a skilled performer and improviser. He entered the Imperial Guard Cadet School in 1852. He died in Saint Petersburg on March 28th 1881.

He composed the piano suite *Pictures at an Exhibition* in 1874.

For photo and more information see: http://russia-in-us.com/Music/Opera/mussorgsky.html

Sergei Prokofiev (1891-1953)

This Ukrainian-born composer composed *Peter and the Wolf* for narrator and orchestra in 1934. Prokofiev lived outside his homeland for several years, performing all over the world, but in 1936 settled in Moscow. Very soon he experienced governmental disfavour of music that did not suit Joseph Stalin's political and social aims.

Prokofiev composed music for *Romeo and Juliet*, which was to be performed as a ballet in Russia. However, the aftermath of the Great Purge led to the rejection of the composer's ballet. It was later (1938) taken up by the Bolshoi Theatre.

More information at: www.bbc.co.uk/music/profiles/prokofiev.shtml

Franz Schubert (1797-1828)

Franz Schubert was born in Vienna and belonged to a large family. He was the twelfth child, although many of his siblings died in infancy. When he was five years old he started music lessons with his older brother. His father was a schoolmaster who, together with a local teacher, taught him music. His ability was soon beyond them. He joined the Imperial Court Chapel Choir as a boy soprano until his voice broke and he himself trained to became a teacher. In 1815, while working as primary teacher, he composed about 150 songs including *Erlkönig, symphonies 2 & 3*, four operas, two masses and other works. He then started to compose in earnest, eventually giving up teaching altogether so that he could devote even more time to his music.

Everything we know about Schubert suggests that he was a quiet and private man. He was a skilled pianist and violinist but many of his orchestra compositions were never performed publicly, and only his chamber music and songs were able to be performed in smaller social gatherings. Because of this Schubert was quite poor. His music was not so well known at the time. It was not until after his death that others started to recognise his genius. Some of his works were then published and performed for the first time, and gradually his talents became widely recognised. During his short lifetime the lack of widespread public awareness didn't seem to bother him. He seemed driven to spend his time composing, and he relied on the feedback and support of a small circle of friends and admirers instead of public acclaim.

Schubert's Piano Quintet is called *The Trout* because the slow movement is a set of variations on the theme of the song of that name.

More information from www.mfiles.co.uk/composers/Franz-Schubert.htm and http://myweb.tiscali.co.uk/franzschubert/life/time.html

Peter Ilyich Tchaikovsky (1840-1893)

He was born in Russia. He was given piano lessons at the age of five and within a year it is said he could play better than his teacher. When he was 19 he worked in an office and studied music in his spare time. Four years later he became a student at the St Petersburg Conservatory, graduating with honours and offered a post at the Moscow Conservatory. One of his admirers was a wealthy widow who, in 1877, gave him a pension (a yearly sum of money) so that he could work without worrying about money; though they never met they exchanged over 3,000 letters. She was his pen-friend for 14 years and their letters tell us a great deal about his thoughts and feelings about his music. He composed the *Romeo and Juliet Fantasy Overture* as well as ballets such as *Swan Lake* and *The Nutcracker*. The ballet *The Sleeping Beauty* was first performed by the Imperial Ballet at the Maryinsky Theatre, St Petersburg, in 1890. He also composed the beautiful *Serenade for Strings* and the stirring *1812 Overture* with cannonfire for sound effects.

More information at: www.pianoparadise.com/Tchaikovsky.html

Appendix 2:

Ballet and other stories

Coppelia

This story was written by Charles Nuitter and Arthur Saint-Leon from a story by E A Hoffmann. Leo Delibes composed the first performance at the Opera in Paris in 1870.

The story of Coppelia is as follows:

Dr Coppelius was a toymaker who made mechanical life-size dolls and lived in his house and workshop with his daughter Coppelia. Every day Coppelia sat on the balcony reading, but never moved or spoke. She even ignored Swanhilda, the friendliest girl in the village, who tried to make her speak.

Swanhilda's boyfriend was Franz, who loved her dearly and wanted to marry her, but one day she caught him blowing kisses to Coppelia and this made Swanhilda very angry.

The lord of the village was to give a new bell to the village and this was to be rung for the first time the next day for all the new brides. The burgomaster asked if Swanhilda was to be one of them but she was angry with Franz so shook her head and ran off.

That evening several small boys were messing about outside Dr Coppelius' house when he went out. He set about them with his cane and chased them away. As he did so, he didn't notice that he had dropped the key to his house. When Swanhilda and her friends came back they found the key. Swanhilda said she was going to go into the workshop and talk to Coppelia, but her friends shook their heads. However, they followed her into the house…

Just then Franz came to the house with a ladder – he was going to see Coppelia too and placed the ladder against the window.

In the workshop Swanhilda and her friends met Coppelia face to face, but she wouldn't notice or talk to them. As they got nearer they realised that Coppelia wasn't a girl at all, but a life-size doll. The girls then began to play with all the musical toys in the workshop and set them all working. They danced among the toys and had a wonderful time, until Dr Coppelius suddenly came home! He was angry at them and shouted to them to get out. They all ran away except Swanhilda who hid behind the curtain in the window where the doll Coppelia was sitting.

Then Franz came up the ladder into the workshop and asked Dr Coppelius if he could marry his daughter not knowing that she was just a doll. Dr Coppelius asked Franz to have a drink with him, but also filled his glass with a magic potion.

Franz fell asleep and Dr Coppelius set to work. He pushed Coppelia's chair into the centre of the room and got out his magic book. He drew energy from Franz's eyes, muscles and bones and thrust it at Coppelia. Coppelia began to smile and then started to breathe. Her eyes blinked, her shoulders moved and she stood up and took a few steps. Poor Dr Coppelius didn't know that Swanhilda had changed clothes with the doll Coppelia and was pretending to be her. He really thought that his doll had come to life. Coppelia danced faster and faster and then became tired. She noticed Franz in the corner, fast asleep and tried to wake him. Then she started winding up all the toys and dolls and they began to dance again. Dr Coppelius didn't know what to do with all the dolls out of control. He pleaded with Coppelia to be good, but she seized Franz's hand and ran out into the street leaving Dr Coppelius in despair next to his doll Coppelia who had never come to life at all.

Next day all the villagers came to listen to the new bell. Swanhilda and Franz led a procession of brides and grooms, but just as the burgomaster was thanking the lord for the new bell, Dr Coppelius came across the square. He had wrapped Coppelia in a blanket and brought her from the workshop. He was very angry and wanted an explanation from the young people of the village. Swanhilda and Franz begged him to forgive them for their trick, and Swanhilda asked him to take her dowry to make up for it. Dr Coppelius forgave her at once and when the burgomaster gave Dr Coppelius a bag of gold coins he stopped being angry, gave the gold back, smiled at everyone and went back to his workshop.

Franz hugged Swanhilda and promised to love her forever, saying that a doll was not as good as a real bride. He said he would give his heart to Swanhilda and promised always to be faithful to her. She accepted him and so they were married.

Nutcracker

Composed by Tchaikovsky and based on a German story by E T A Hoffmann. The first performance was in Maryinsky Theatre St Petersburg in 1892.

The story is as follows:

Clara and her little brother Fritz had a big party on Christmas Eve. The children could hardly wait to open their presents under the big Christmas tree. Clara's godfather, Drosselmeyer, and his nephew came in to bring their presents. He turned keys that set three toy people dancing, before they were taken away to keep them safe. Clara and Drosselmeyer's nephew quickly became friends and played together. Her godfather then gave Clara a special present – a painted wooden soldier that was really a nutcracker. He showed her how it worked. She thanked him for the present and then little Fritz grabbed it, dropped it and it broke on the floor. Her godfather bandaged the wooden nutcracker's head with a handkerchief and said it would be better soon so Clara put it into one of her doll's beds for the night. Then all the other children went home, Fritz was sent to bed and Clara kissed her nutcracker good night and went to bed herself.

Later that night Clara crept downstairs to see that the nutcracker was safe. The room seemed different; the Christmas tree seemed to grow larger and began to shine. Then huge mice came to her and she cried for help. Fritz's toy soldiers, now life-sized, came to attention and rushed to help. The nutcracker sprang to life, leapt to his feet and charged into the battle fighting the Mouse King. The nutcracker was brave, but stumbled; Clara took off her slipper to throw at King Mouse and the nutcracker speared him with his sword. The mice all ran away, taking their king with them. The nutcracker vanished too and in his place stood her godfather's nephew, dressed as a prince. He put the Mouse King's crown on Clara's head and led her away into the snowy night.

They went to the land of the sweets, walking along toffee pathways until they came to the palace of the Sugar Plum Fairy. 'Thank you for coming,' she said. 'Was it a difficult journey?' They told her about the Mouse King's battle and how Clara had helped to defeat him with her shoe. The Sugar Plum Fairy told them to rest a while on her wonderful throne. Then she asked for all her sweets to come and dance for them.

All the different kinds of toffees and sweets and chocolates came to dance. Chocolate did a fiery Spanish dance, Chinese Tea bowed again and again to the children and Russian peppermints tumbled and danced everywhere. Next, Mother Ginger appeared with her children all around her before the candied flowers danced in. Then the Sugar Plum Fairy came back with her own handsome prince. They, too, danced for the children. Clara kissed the Sugar Plum Fairy and thanked all the dancers before taking her prince's hand and leaving the land of the sweets.

There are different endings to this ballet – sometimes Clara wakes up in her own bed and thinks it was just a dream; sometimes she waves goodbye to them and rides off with her prince into the future on a golden sleigh.

For more information and photographs, see www.radacadabra.org/nutcracker.htm

Swan Lake

Tchaikovsky first performed this in Moscow 1887. A new version was choreographed and performed in 1895 at the Maryinsky Theatre St Petersburg.

The story is as follows:

Prince Siegfried and the queen lived in a great stone castle. Every year there was a party for his friends and everyone else in the village. When it was his coming-of-age party the queen gave him a crossbow for a present. Then she said that he was now old enough to become king and that it was time he got married. She said she had invited many lovely ladies to a grand ball the next evening and he must choose his bride before the end of the ball.

Siegfried was very upset, but his friend Benno said that he could enjoy himself that day. As a flock of swans flew up into the sky Benno said it would be a good time to try his new crossbow and so Siegfried organised a hunt.

The hunt party came to a lake in the deepest part of the forest and saw the swans there. As Siegfried got ready to aim one of the swans came towards him and suddenly turned into a beautiful young lady. She said she was Odette the Queen of the swans and that an evil sorcerer Rothbart had cast a spell on her and all the swans. The swans could only return to human form at night, between midnight and dawn. She begged Siegfried not to shoot them.

Siegfried asked how he could help to break the spell, and Odette said that only when someone fell in love with her, promised that he would never love anyone else and would marry her would the spell be broken. Siegfried said he was already in love with her and would always be faithful.

But the wicked wizard Rothbart was hiding watching them and when the dawn came he ordered them back to the lake. She tried to resist but the magic was too strong and all the swans flew off into the sky.

Siegfried was very unhappy especially when it was time for the ball. Many beautiful princesses were there and all wanted him to marry them, but he could only think of Odette. The queen said he must choose one of the princesses as his bride, but the prince refused. Suddenly it went dark and thunder roared. Two strangers appeared. One was Rothbart, disguised as a count and the other his daughter Odile disguised as Odette.

Siegfried thought that Odette had come to be with him and they danced wondrously together; he didn't notice the real Odette fluttering at the window. Siegfried told everyone that he would marry Odile and that he would love her always. At that moment Rothbart laughed and said that Siegfried had broken his promise and that now Odette would belong to him forever. He put his cloak around Odile and they disappeared.

Siegfried realised that he had been tricked and rushed out of the ballroom to try to find Odette.

Odette returned to the swans in the forest; they all tried to console her, saying that Siegfried would come to her, but Odette said she could not bear the enchantment any more and would rather die.

Just then Siegfried dashed in and embraced her, vowing eternal love, but Rothbart appeared and said that he would never release her. He attacked the prince, who fought valiantly trying to save Odette. As Rothbart stumbled, Odette rushed to Siegfried, kissed him one last time before climbing the rocks and throwing herself into the lake. Siegfried couldn't bear to lose her and followed her to his death.

Thus Rothbart's powerful magic was destroyed and he collapsed into a heap of feathers, releasing the swan maidens from the spell.

La Fille mal Gardee by Ferdinand Herold

This ballet is about a girl whose old mother (usually played by a man) tries to keep her safe on their farm. The girl keeps trying to get away from her chores to be with her boyfriend and other village farm boys. This boyfriend is not at all rich and the old mother tries to keep them apart. Even though the mother tries all kinds of ways to keep her away from him, the two plan to marry.

The mother finds a rich husband for her daughter and arranges to sign papers to organise a marriage, but the daughter and the boyfriend are in an upper room arranging their own marriage. However, when the mother sees how determined her daughter is to have her own way, she agrees to their marriage and it all ends happily. The clog dance is about half way through the ballet, when the old mother dances in her clogs with the music getting faster and faster until she almost falls over.

Peter and the Wolf

Peter lived with his grandfather in a cottage in a wide green meadow, near a dark, mysterious forest. In the garden was a tall tree and Peter thought that if he climbed it he would be able to see the whole of the meadow, the duck pond and part of the forest. Grandfather warned Peter not to play in the meadow because of the wolf that lived in the forest. He told Peter that the wolf might come and gobble him up.

But Peter wasn't afraid of the wolf and decided to disobey Grandfather. As he skipped into the meadow he heard a bird singing and twittering and then he saw a duck in the middle of the pond. The duck was quacking and it seemed as though it was having an argument with the bird. The bird was saying that it was better than a duck because he could fly, but the duck said that he was better because he could swim.

While they quarrelled, Peter noticed a hungry looking cat creeping closer to the pond. Peter shouted to alert the bird, who flew to a branch on the tree and mocked the cat, who couldn't catch him. Peter was happy that he had saved the bird, but then he suddenly heard Grandfather shouting angrily. 'What are you doing in the meadow?' he shouted. 'Have you forgotten about the wolf?'

Grandfather took hold of Peter and took him back into the garden.

Then Peter noticed a wolf creeping through the grass towards the cat which had fallen asleep. The wolf looked very hungry as he crept nearer and nearer.

Suddenly the bird noticed the wolf and started to chirp. This woke the cat up and he fled up the tree. But the duck wasn't as quick as the cat and in no time the wolf had gobbled him up.

Peter decided he would try to catch the wolf; he grabbed a rope and climbed up the tall tree in the garden. He tied one end of the rope to a branch overhanging the meadow and the other end into a lasso. He told the bird to try to lure the wolf towards the rope, so the bird flew around the wolf's head, teasing him, calling, 'Can't catch me!'

This made the wolf angry and he chased after the bird getting nearer and nearer to the tree. As the wolf passed under one of the overhanging branches Peter let down the rope and caught the wolf's tail in the lasso.

He called to his Grandfather that he had caught the wolf and just then a band of huntsmen came out of the forest. They aimed their rifles at the wolf to shoot him but Peter shouted, 'Don't shoot, we can take him to the zoo.'

Grandfather was happy that the wolf had been caught and there was a great celebration as the huntsmen paraded through the town taking the wolf to the zoo.

The Gingerbread Man

A little old man and a little old woman were very sad that they didn't have a child. One day the little old woman made a little boy out of gingerbread. She put him into the oven to cook. Soon they heard a voice shouting from the oven, 'Let me out, let me out,' and when they opened the oven door a little Gingerbread Man jumped out and ran across the floor, through the door and into the wide, wide world. The little old man and the little old woman called to the Gingerbread Man to stop, but he wouldn't. He just called over his shoulder, 'Run! Run! As fast as you can, you can't catch me, I'm the Gingerbread Man.'

A cow noticed the Gingerbread Man as he ran through the meadow and he called, 'Stop, I want to eat you up.' But the Gingerbread Man went on running and he just called over his shoulder, 'Run! Run! As fast as you can, you can't catch me, I'm the Gingerbread Man.'

A horse saw the Gingerbread Man and shouted, 'Stop, I want to eat you up.' But the Gingerbread Man went on running and he just called over his shoulder, 'Run! Run! As fast as you can, you can't catch me, I'm the Gingerbread Man.'

A schoolboy and girl saw the Gingerbread Man and shouted, 'Stop, we want to eat you up.' But the Gingerbread Man went on running and he just called over his shoulder 'Run! Run! As fast as you can, you can't catch me, I'm the Gingerbread Man.'

A dog woke up as the Gingerbread Man ran past and he called, 'Stop, I want to eat you up.' But the Gingerbread Man went on running and he just called over his shoulder, 'Run! Run! As fast as you can, you can't catch me, I'm the Gingerbread Man.'

A cat spied the Gingerbread Man and shouted, 'Stop, I want to eat you up.' But the Gingerbread Man went on running and he just called over his shoulder, 'Run! Run! As fast as you can, you can't catch me, I'm the Gingerbread Man.'

The Gingerbread Man kept on running away from the little old man and the little old woman, from the cow, the horse, the children, the dog and the cat and not one of them could catch him.

Just then he came to a river and had to stop. How could he get across without getting wet and soggy? Just then he heard a sly little voice, 'I'll help you across.' It was a sly old fox who tricked the Gingerbread Man to get onto his tail to cross the river.

The Gingerbread Man's feet got wet so he moved onto the fox's back, then onto his head and finally onto his nose, as all the fox's body except his nose was under the water as he swam fast to the other side.

The Gingerbread Man thought he was safe until the fox threw back his head and tossed the Gingerbread Man into the air and snapped his jaws.

'Oh dear, I'm a quarter gone,' said the Gingerbread Man.

The fox snapped again. 'Oh dear, I'm half gone,' said the Gingerbread Man. The fox snapped again. 'Oh dear I am three-quarters gone,' said the Gingerbread Man. The fox snapped again. And the Gingerbread Man said nothing at all because he was all gone.

But that's what gingerbread men are made for after all.

The Wild Swans

A princess, Elisa, had eleven brothers. Her father married a wicked queen who sent Elisa away from the palace and cast a spell on the eleven brothers turning them into swans. When Elisa was fifteen she returned to the palace and the queen hated her because she was beautiful. She used magic to make Elisa ugly and the king turned her out. Elisa wandered through the country until one day she met an old woman who told her about eleven swans with golden crowns. Elisa found eleven white feathers on the beach and waited until the sun set when eleven swans landed nearby and changed into eleven handsome princes. They were overjoyed to see her. They told her that in the day they had to be swans and lived across the sea, but at night they changed back into princes. Elisa persuaded them to take her back with them so they wove a basket to carry her and when dawn came they started across the sea. It was hard for them to carry her and a great storm blew up. They put her down on a very small rock in the sea just as the sun set and the swans changed into princes. The rock was so small that they had to huddle together in the terrible storm. In the morning the swans carried her back to their home in a cave. Elisa dreamed of the old woman who told Elisa that she could break the spell if she would knit shirts from nettles to throw them over the princes. There was one condition, if she spoke even one word the princes would die. When she awoke she started collecting nettles and began to knit. A young king came by, noticed her and thought he had never seen such a beautiful girl. Elisa remembered that she must not speak. The king took her to his palace and dressed her in royal robes and married her but some people said that she was a witch. Every night she gathered nettles in the churchyard and knitted shirts out of them. The king heard about this and followed her. When he saw her gathering nettles he, too, thought she must be a witch and put her in prison and said she would be killed as a witch the next day.

The swan princes heard about this and went to see the king but the servants refused to let them in. When the king heard about this it was already dawn and he saw eleven swans flying over the palace.

The next day Elisa was to be killed as a witch and many people came to see. They tried to take the nettle shirts but eleven swans flew down and settled around her. Their wings beat back the crowd and Elisa threw the shirts over them and they became eleven handsome princes – all except the eleventh whose shirt sleeve was not quite finished and so he still had a swan's wing as an arm. The princes told the story to the king and Elisa could now speak again. She told the king that she loved him so they all lived happily ever after in the king's palace.

Appendix 3:

Music notation

The Elephant Song

Spanish Folk Song

One e-le-phant went out to play on a san-dy beach one day.

She ha-d such en-or-mous fun that she called for an-oth-er e-lephant to come.

Days of the Week

Traditional Somerset Song

T'was on a Mon- day mor - ning When I be-held my dar - ling She

looked so sweet and char - ming In ev - ery high deg-ree. She looked so neat and nim - ble-o A

wash - ing of her lin - en o. Dash - ing - a - way with the smoo - thing iron.

Dash - ing a - way with the smoo - thing iron. She stole my hea rt a way.

Tuesday - a hanging out her linen-o
Wednesday - a drying of her linen-o
Thursday - an ironing of her linen-o
Friday - an airing of her linen-o
Saturday - a folding of her linen-o
Sunday - a wearing of her linen-o

Appendix 4: Resources

Venezia, M. (Series) *Getting to Know the World's Greatest Composers*. London: Franklin Watts Ltd.

Kendall, A. (2000) *The Chronicle of Classical Music*. London: Thames and Hudson Ltd.

Newman, B. (2005) *The Illustrated Book of Ballet Stories*. London: Dorling Kindersley.

Geras, A. & Beck, I. (2000) *The Orchard Book of Opera Stories*. London: Orchard Books.

Jessop, J. (1993) *Famous Musicians*. Hove: Wayland Publishers. (OOP)

Song/music books

Foss, P. & Turner, B.C. (1989) *Oranges and Lemons, Castanets and Scrapers*.

International Music Publications.

King, K. (1986) *Oranges and Lemons*. Oxford: Oxford University Press.

Riordan, J. (1986) *Peter and the Wolf*. Oxford: Oxford University Press.

Powell, H. (2001) *Game-Songs with Prof Dogg's Troupe*. London: A&C Black.

Gadsby, D. (2002) *Flying a Round*. London: A&C Black.

Piccolo Book of Favourite Songs (1991) Pan Books.

Marks, A. & Cartwright, S. (1997) *The Usborne Children's Song Book*. Usborne Publishing.

Harop, B. (Ed.) (1996) *Apusskidu*. London: A&C Black.

Picture storybooks

Axtell, D. (2000) *We're Going on a Lion Hunt*. London: Macmillan Children's Books.

Anderson, H.C. & Monozumi, A. (Illustrator) (2003) *The Wild Swans*. Matthew Price Publishing.

Browne, E. (1995) *Handa's Surprise*. London: Walker Books.

Browne, E. (2003) *Handa's Hen*. London: Walker Books.

Hull, R. & Allsopp, K. (Illustrator) (2000) *Stories From West Africa*. London: Hodder Wayland.

Circle Time books

Collins, M. (2001) *Circle Time for the Very Young*. London: Paul Chapman Publishing.

Collins, M. (2002) *Circling Round Citizenship*. London: Paul Chapman Publishing.

Collins, M. (2002) *Because I'm Special.* London: Paul Chapman Publishing.

Collins, M. (2003) *Enhancing Circle Time for the Very Young.* London: Paul Chapman Publishing.

Collins, M (2004) *Circling Safely.* London: Paul Chapman Publishing.

More useful websites

http://www.dfes.gov.uk/musicservices

National Curriculum: http://www.nc.uk.net/

www.rhymes.org.uk